POEMS OF AMERICAN LIFE

POEMS

OF

AMERICAN
LIFE

᠎᠎᠎᠎᠎᠎᠎᠎᠎᠎᠎᠎᠎᠎᠎᠎᠎᠎᠎᠎᠎᠎᠎᠎᠎᠎᠎᠎᠎᠎᠎᠎᠎᠎᠎᠎᠎᠎᠎

MERRILL MOORE

᠎᠎᠎᠎᠎᠎᠎᠎᠎᠎᠎᠎᠎᠎᠎᠎᠎᠎᠎᠎᠎᠎᠎᠎᠎᠎᠎᠎᠎᠎᠎᠎᠎᠎᠎᠎᠎᠎᠎

With an Introduction
by
Louis Untermeyer

PHILOSOPHICAL LIBRARY

NEW YORK

MERRILL MOORE: 1903-1957

Merrill Moore was barely twenty, an undergraduate at Vanderbilt University, when, after a couple of lectures, I got to know him in Nashville. He was the youngest member of a little group that called itself *The Fugitive* and published a magazine of the same name. The group, which signed their contributions with fancy pseudonyms, included John Crowe Ransom ("Roger Prim"), Allen Tate ("Henry Feathertop"), Donald Davidson ("Robin Gallivant") and Merrill ("Dendric")—Robert Penn Warren, two years Merrill's junior, was a later member. Looking back through the mist of more than thirty years, I see that I contributed to the second number of *The Fugitive,* along with Merrill and the Nashvillians.

That was in 1922. His fellow Fugitives—it never was made clear what they were trying to escape—already recognized Merrill as a prodigy who was also a problem. At pre-publication sessions, each one submitted a poem, which was freely criticized, and presented at the next meeting in a revised version. It was a procedure which was followed by everyone except Merrill. Every criticism set up a chain reaction in Merrill's mind and instead of bringing an improved poem to the next session, Merrill submitted a dozen wholly new, and obviously improvised, sonnets.

He was already writing sonnets as a freshman, and in the thirty-five ensuing years, he wrote practically nothing but sonnets. His work grew by proliferation instead of by accretion. By the time he was twenty-six and his first volume, *The Noise That Time Makes,* had appeared, it was rumored that Merrill had composed close to ten thousand sonnets and that he was learning shorthand in order to get his fourteen-liners down on paper faster. I laughed at this. But after I had helped Merrill edit two more volumes—one of which was severely entitled *M* because, besides being Merrill's initials, it contained one thousand sonnets—I made a rough inventory of the manuscripts he had stored in filing cabinets in Springfield Street, Boston. There were, give or take five hundred, close to forty thousand sonnets.

Astonishing though this figure may be, it is, having known Merrill, not incredible. He told me that since his eighteenth year he had written an average of five sonnets a day and, though there were days when he held himself down to a single example of the form, he had bursts of free association which went on until he had accumulated enough pages for another volume. On one occasion, he said, he had written as many as one hundred in four hours—he said he timed himself. The sonnets were like no one else's—free-rhyming, impromptu, and wholly American in their conversational tone.

Meanwhile, after working his way through medical school by teaching French, he had become a psychiatrist, had married, and had emigrated to Boston. There he instructed at the Harvard Medical School and pursued his researches—largely in the problems of alcoholism and attempted suicide—at the Boston City and Boston Psychopathic Hospitals. In his non-poetic function, he published more than a hundred medical papers, including one with the deceptively idyllic title of "Syphilis and Sassafras." During World War Two, he volunteered for medical work with the army and served in the war area of the Pacific for four years, from 1942 to 1946. He spent much of the time in the hospitals of New Zealand and in China, where he was associated with General Wedemeyer and was designated Consultant with the Military Advisory Group there. He bore the rank of Major when he was discharged from active duty; each summer thereafter he spent two weeks in camp as a reserve medical officer.

For the last ten years, Merrill gave himself equally to poetry and psychiatry. His patients and his poems continued to grow in arithmetical progression. One thing led to another—or, to be more exact, one patient led to a dozen sonnets, for the poetry became more and more like condensed case histories. Countless other poets wrote sonnets; Merrill *thought* in them. I always meant to measure his talk, for I was sure that his conversation would fall into units of fourteen lines. When he built a new two-story house—one floor for consultations, and one to house his sonnets—it was obvious that it should be called his Sonnetorium.

Nor were Merrill's incalculable energies limited to creation and therapy. A Protean person, he was an athlete—for years he competed in the twelve-mile swimming race from Charlestown to Boston Light—a great walker, and a passionate gardener. He not only loved to make over his own garden and everyone else's—including mine—but he was seen in coveralls putting in small trees in front of his office on Commonwealth Avenue. The scope of his correspondence was international, the range of his interests universal. An unprofessional documentary photographer, he seems to have made as many pictures as sonnets—his collection of Pacific photographs, when edited, will constitute a poet's-eye-record of a vast area. Collecting shells in Florida, he became a devoted conchologist, and urged many of his patients to study the infinite variety of shells as a sublimation of certain maladjustments. One of his citations mentioned his "untiring energy, zeal, and enthusiasm"—qualities which turned casual acquaintances into constant friends throughout the world. When he became ill in the summer of 1957, his family were continually answering telephone calls from every part of the globe.

A man who never seemed to weaken or indulge himself in a passing headache, Merrill went to the hospital in July to be examined for what seemed nothing more than a low fever. On August 1st, when he was operated upon, it was discovered that he was suffering from intestinal cancer and that the liver was largely involved. Completely aware that he was dying, he came home to be taken care of by his family—his wife, his three sons (two of whom have had medical training) and his daughter —and to make plans for his literary properties and the transferring of his patients. Seven weeks after the operation he died peacefully, September 20, 1957, nine days after his fifty-fourth birthday. America had lost one of its most individual poets, and I had lost my closest friend.

LOUIS UNTERMEYER
Great Hill Road
Newtown, Connecticut

The Poems

POEMS OF AMERICAN LIFE

Green Trousdale and Same Sevier

The deference these old men showed each other
Was a wall of granite it took years to build
Stone by stone and if you stop to consider
That it was no other beast than Time that killed
The lack of respect that once roved free between them
You should not marvel that their eyes were dim
When finally the stone wall was erected
And all the primal errors were corrected.

They were no different then from two locust trees
With a wall between them of stone, one on either side;

Both stretched out their branches to heaven in pride
Giving honey to a thousand bees,

Both shed their old leaves early in the fall
But always between them was the granite wall.

Old Men and Old Women Going Home on the Street Car

🔲🔲🔲

Carrying their packages of groceries in particular
With books under their arms that maybe they will read
And possibly understand, old women lead
Their weaker selves up to the front of the car.

And old men who for thirty years have sat at desks
Survey them harmlessly.
                                      They regard each other
As forgotten sister looks at forgotten brother
On their way between two easily remembered tasks
And that is positively all there is to it.

But it was not that way thirty years ago!
Before desks and counters had tired their backs and
      feet,

When life for them was a bowl of odorous fruit
That they might take their pick of, then turn and go
Saying, "This tastes so good!" or, "This smells so
      sweet!"

Abschied

And . . . after the dance was over he
Went up to the ones who were sitting in the car
And told them all how much he'd like to be
Invited again and whistled them a bar
Of music from the song he'd liked the best,
The one they played while he had danced and she
Had remarked what everyone wore, how each was
    dressed;
And they all agreed and laughed contentedly.

But somehow he felt as far away by then
As if instead of the car he peered into
He were a hunter looking into a pit
Where, thick-furred, in the dark were one or two
Fierce bears whose sharp claws tore, whose white teeth
    bit
The flesh that chanced unarmed to fall within.

Antwort

There are three ways to get your answer to me:

One, loose your pigeons, for they know my roof;
Tie the message on one with a tiny band
And it will bring but will not understand
The words that she who holds herself aloof
Has written on rice paper with black ink.

That is the quickest way to do it, I think,
Others I know, but none as instantly.

Or tie a ribbon on the white swan's neck;
Red for yes and ocean-blue for no,
They pass by here to water.
                              If they go
Three days unribboned I'll know that you walk
In your rose garden waiting for the Fall
To tell me by blowing dead leaves over my wall.

Public Park: Roué on a Bench

He is an old roué, rather old,
But not too old to fail to recognize scorn
From a young girl not especially interested in gold
But more in youths that consider themselves forlorn.

Young girls have eyes especially for arms that move
Quickly and gracefully about what they do;
Eyes need be fresh, not necessarily blue.

Similar details determine that sort of love
Which the young enact very largely in public parks
Conveniently far from street-lights and their glow
But conveniently near to fountains whose quiet flow
Is enough to float their intimate craft that embarks
On a sea it does not know the meaning of
But is quite content simply to name it love.

How She Resolved to Act

"I shall be careful to say nothing at all
About myself or what I know of him
Or the vaguest thought I have—no matter how dim,
Tonight if it so happen that he call."
And not ten minutes later the door-bell rang
And into the hall he stepped as he always did
With a face and a bearing that quite poorly hid
His brain that burned and his heart that fairly sang

And his tongue that wanted to be rid of the truth.
As well as she could, for she was very loath
To signify how she felt, she kept very still,
But soon her heart cracked loud as a coffee mill
And her brain swung like a comet in the dark
And her tongue raced like a squirrel in the park.

Candidate for High Office in the Land

His name is a long symphony that a thousand men
Have practiced over and over and over again
For many days to make it magnificent
When it is presented in a public place.

His name is that, but such is not his face;
It is a paper bag in which are pent
A wasp, a bee and a butterfly together
Longing to be out in the summer weather.

So, as we hear his high name being played,
We look on his low face and are not dismayed
By the thunderous notes its syllables suggest

And we are assured that the mystic hand knew best
That twisted the neck of the bag so that the bee,
The wasp and the butterfly never should be free.

Old Men

Talking about men who are richer than they are
And telling how things that are might be otherwise
And looking out of the corners of their eyes
Are what old men inordinately like to do,

Men not so old that they have lost all care
For matters they used to pride themselves about
But certainly long since past the finding out
Of whether these matters were or were not true.

And there are some old men who are scrupulously clean
And some who have kept a fragment of the days
That were broken when Time crashed their shelf to the
    ground,

These old men are neither fat nor lean,
Nor short nor tall; they are distinguishable by the ways
They light their pipes and suddenly turn around.

The Trouble

The trouble with this lady is that she
Will not admire the rose but she will say
"Who planted it?" and learning turn away.

For blackamoors, though suppliant on the knee,
Never appealed to her, even when sublimed
Into lovely rose-plants that they set and tended
Against the seasons' buffetings unended
Through the cold nights when steeple-bells had chimed
Not as cold, though they were made of brass,
As the lady's tongue that would not let feeling pass
From her timid heart whose small doors shut because

The sweetness was removed from a lovely rose
That had been tended by a blackamoor
Rich in roses, otherwise rather poor.

Idiomatische Sprache

"Rather than acknowledge this question as debatable
I would open my tables to your laws
First crying loudly, 'Give me the first cause
And I will answer any question you ask
Bordering honestly on the appointed task,'
But as for those loose ends and worn-out strings,
Cast them among the other outworn things
That cannot even generously be called statable."

Senators were speaking thus and I wondered on
The meaning of such mighty gusts of wind,
For surely the wind means much as it passes by;

Now I discount widely the wind's cry
Hearing it shrilly repeated *the wind has sinned*
And these are the evils that are pondered on.

Mr. and Mrs. Alonzo Sidney

People of that sort seem to attract each other
About as cattle manage to find the clover
That only grows sparsely in a pasture field
And miss the rich black spots of earth that yield
Always the greenest and most luscious grass.

No one can say just how it comes to pass
Any more than one might try to explain how it happens
That breaks occur in fences where gold grain ripens.

They pass each other one day in the street
Without introduction, without fore-knowledge at all

Or they may see each other at a ball
And chance to inquire and the next day they meet.

Then the game begins that takes the rest of their life;
Man and woman, parents, husband and wife.

Lucky Strike

Those who have no agent paid to cry
Their story loudly in the public ear,
To write their names in smoke across the sky
And advertise their moan, applaud their tear
And dwell upon their nature's worthiness
Are fortunate in this:

                                    it seems that they
Are let to live a little longer than
The uppermost, who are uppermost for a day
But then they see a long descent begin
That terminates in a mystic dismalness
Where old forgotten songs are half-way heard

And unused clothes, bought for children who died,
Lie rumpled on a cold eternal floor
That women sweep, who never swept before.

Aaron Daniel

Aaron is getting old and quicker to feel,
Now than ever before, Winter's approach.

It is no longer a subject that I dare broach
And one that harasses him certainly a great deal
To see the long rows of maples before his house
About the time that grain is stacked in sheaves
Slowly begin to lose their rattling leaves
When the meadows are turned over to the mole and
    mouse.

Even his high-stepping horse disdains him now
For Aaron is getting old and his thin calves
Would barely make today respectable halves
Of the ones with which he used to scrape and bow
And dance as steadily as the young ones there
Before the black turned to thin grey in his hair.

Shot Who? Jim Lane!

When he was shot he toppled to the ground
As if the toughened posts that were his thighs
Had felt that all that held them up were lies,

Weak lies, that suddenly someone had found
Out all that was true about them.
                                    It did not seem
Like the crashing of a stalwart forest oak
But like a frail staff that a sharp wind broke
Or something insubstantial in a dream.

I never thought Jim Lane would fall like that.

He'd sworn that bullets must be gold to find him;
That when they came toward him he made them mind
        him
By means he knew,
                    just as a barn-yard cat
Can keep a pack of leaping dogs at bay
By concentrating and looking a certain way.

Undergraduate

He dreamed of lovely women as he slept,
Women with slim white legs and long white arms
And soft round breasts, the two moons of his night.

And as he rolled and tossed on his narrow bed
He dreamed that the arms were slipped beneath his
    head,
And under his neck, while women's lovely forms
Like marble urns surrounded him and kept
A silent watch that disappeared when light
Began to tinge the sky and paint the wall
With colors it had never had at all,

And the marble vases that were women where
The dreams had stood were melted into air

And all the arms that had clasped and held his head
Were twisted sheets and feather-pillows instead.

The Anger of Mr. Northcutt

He had the power of throwing an invisible wall
About himself that inclosed him from head to foot,
An impassable partition no one could put
One finger through, were he displeased at all.

The moment any one said the slightest thing
That made his ears point back the slightest bit
That wall appeared, and he, enclosed in it,
Would look out at us as if he scorned to fling
The venom of his eyes in our direction.

It was just as though a great cylinder of glass
Large enough to contain a man were placed
Down over his body, and he was poison-faced
Whenever an incautious word would pass
The lips of those he eyed as for correction.

The Tarver House I

Though the huge house stood empty on the hill
And dark, where dozens of lamps had made windows
     flare
Yellowly out on summer and winter air
The nights when all the people were alive
Who used to live there, and though it was still,
Still as when bees are all asleep in a hive,

On certain nights when the wind became too odorous
Or when the rain-beat grew too dolorous

A change occurred within its silent walls
That allowed the ghosts of the dead former tenants
That slept in the walls to slip out into the halls
And the great front rooms and there begin a dance
Till the house was overcrowded;
                     so many men
And so many women had lived there since eighteen-ten.

The Tarver House II

It was not necessary for the rats and mice
In that house to use the brass locks and keys
As the mortals that dwelt in it had to use,

Keys and rings were far too easy to lose.

There were holes that were large enough to squeeze
Through in an instant, some of them were twice
As large as the largest rat might need to slip
Into if he heard an approaching step

And every corner of the floor-board had
One and two and sometimes a triad
Of places gnawed completely through the door
And through the plaster level with the floor,

Even the edges of the doors were chiselled away
By the teeth of the rats that ran through every day.

Grey Roofs

Under these grey roofs Misery dwells
With an eye that burns and a pointed tooth that gnaws

And for no other apparent cause
Than that the goods she buys and the wares she sells
Can be bought and sold at places conveniently near:

Shops where withered faces are for sale
And stores where young soft hands tell an eager tale
Of hope that never ends and wonder and fear.

These roofs shelter the shops where Misery makes
All the articles she carries in trade,

It is at slight cost that they are made
And very quickly,
                          Misery only takes
A little while to put this and that together
So it will stand up under all sorts of weather.

Rana Americana

Come join the frogs, they only jump so high,
They do not look for symbols in the sky.

They do not ask for sustenance beyond
What is afforded by their scummy pond.

Wind does not chill them, they thrive in rainy weather;
At night they croak in harmony together.

King-fishers are strong; snakes are treacherous;
But frog-legs are spry; never timorous.

Some of the tribe are known to live in trees,
(For literature, see Aristophanes.)

Students preserve them in formalin in a bottle;
They have been closely watched by Aristotle.

On them subsists a nation as famous as France,
They do not wear collars, belts or pants.

A Lady Is Buried Here

She will not hear the sea where she is laid
Because the sea beats soft too far below.

"High on a hill-side—" was the prayer she made
Just as she turned her eyes away to go
Beyond the limits of her heart's poor strength
Whose pulsing rose and fell as quietly
As sap flows up or leaves drop from a tree
As the life span reaches its final length.

There in autumn fly the faithful rooks
Each year to pick the beech-mast from her ground,

Chattering to themselves, flying round—
They would remind her, I know, of the books
She read when she was an enchanted child,
The hills, the beech-trees, the rooks and all things wild.

Monte Carlo, 11 Septembre

Though Monte Carlo was a place where men
Like him had very little to see or do
John Potts kept wondering if it were true
That this was Monaco.
                              He took his pen
And sat down in the hotel to write letters
To all his friends whose addresses he could remember
And headed one *Monte Carlo, 11 Septembre*
As the newspaper had it.
                              He tried to shake the fetters
That thinking in terms of discount and overhead
Had fastened to his ankles, heavy as lead.

He tried to tear a heavy mask away
From his face, his eyelids felt as thick as clay
From sitting eight hours a day in the Kelso Bank
Where the light was poor and the air was always rank.

Bulletins

I saw you walking in the crowded street,
Thousands passed you as you went alone,

And you were young but even then the tone
Of your heels hitting the sidewalk as you passed
Told me that your armies all were massed
To attack with your best defense the enemy
And beat him back and make him blow retreat
And let you ring the bells of victory.

But one by one the men of your army fell;
I heard their names announced in the house of death.

And slowly, slowlier you drew your breath.
Then I read your bulletins that tried to tell
How you might be victorious in the spring
While I knew that they could not mean anything.

Bright Faces

And to what high-walled gardens is it that they go
Or to what shuttered rooms that none may see?

Pray not, I beg you not to ask that of me,

For it is a matter about which I know
Not as much as the moles of the gardens above
Or the mice of the shuttered rooms where voices speak
But little else causes the silence to break
Into the pieces of noise that might be called love
If one were cynic enough to examine the faces
Of bright pretty creatures preening themselves before
Mirrors and eagerly listening at the door
For expected steps—
                            any one of a thousand cases
That all show the same facts true that we lament
As the cause of Weltschmerz, sorrow and malcontent.

Lucia and Louis

Only one autumn, only one autumn ago,
They strolled this road in the hills far over the town,
Watching the autumn sky and looking down
On the smokestacks and roofs cluttering the valley
    below.

Then Winter came with his winds, with a wind to blow
The leaves away from the trees on the hill's high crown;
So they ceased their chatting inasmuch as the leaves
    were blown
Over the paths of the hillside they used to know.

Only one autumn between them—they used to scorn
Those not like them, who would not walk out the heights,

Who drudged months full in the town, unwittingly torn
Between bread and beauty and the blood and the brain's
    cold rights.

But each walks a separate street now in fine stealth
Watching the leaves blow down in the street's black filth.

TRADITION OF A YOUNG POET

It Is Winter, I Know

What if small birds are peppering the sky,
Scudding south with the clouds to an ultimate tip on
	lands
Where they may peck worms and slugs from moist
	sands
Rather muddily mixed with salt?
				Or if wind dashes by
Insufferably filled with bird's indeclinable twitter
Not deigning to toy with the oak-twigs that it passes
And treading but lightly on all the delicate grasses
Under trees where crickets are silent, where mad leaves
	flutter?

It is winter, I know, there are too many Nays now con-
	fronting
The obdurate soul that would trick itself into believing
That buds are still ripe, that cells are all ready for
	cleaving;
It can only be winter, winter alone, when blunting
Winds rush over the ice, scattering leaves from their
	weeds
To rattle the sycamore tree's bitter shrivelled seeds.

Just Then the Door

Just then the door decided to close itself.
In walked One, in walked Two, in walked Three.

With the door shut it was impossible for that to be,
You say, but they walked right in through the door.

And One sat down cross-legged on the floor
And the second propped himself against the wall
And Three, chiefly because he was so tall,
Sat down on and let his legs dangle from the shelf.

Then they all spoke, first one, then another,
Every one of them distinctly calling me "brother"

And every one smiling in his ghastly way
As if his eyes contradicted what his mouth would say,

And each one disappeared like whirling smoke
Just about the time the morning broke.

He Made the World as a Toy to Give His Mistress

And she accepted the gift from him not knowing
That in the heart of the world a seed was growing,
Ready that moment to burst its fibrous shell,
That it would level their house, extinguish the fires,
When it was grown, of their hearth, and mute the lyres
That their shepherds plucked to make them sleep
After strenuous days of herding celestial sheep
On the lonely heaths that separate heaven from hell.

Laughing, he tossed her globe spinning in the air:
"Dearest, what a pretty! Throw it to me!"

The Pacific Ocean spilled in the Indian Sea,
The Great Lakes sloshed about and a thousand trees
Were uprooted and drifted like down on a summer
        breeze
Off to the voiceless depths of anywhere.

Helen Told Me What Was in Her Head

It was just about like this, she said:

I was entirely alone in the empty house
And I started thinking this way—suppose a mouse
Or several mice (I fear them very much)
Would think that I was the sort of little girl
That they would like to eat (for you know that there
    are such),
That they would eat me and not leave any sign
Of the arms and legs and body that had been mine!

That was how she became so terrified
That when we reached the house and turned on the light
She was living in a province of the land of fright

And had to be taken upstairs and put to bed,
So that her eyes that were a deep shade of brown
Would stare less widely and normally quiet down.

We Are Sleepy Shepherds We
1400707

If fourteen lines were fourteen hundred lines,
O then I might begin to start to tell
Matters I have thought about until
Both my eyes ache and my incorrigible brain
Answers my will with, "No, I will not sleep,
I'll guard this flock of thoughts lest one escape
And all the others, hearing the strange whines
The wolf forgetfulness makes, will leap the pen
And follow the lost thoughts into the forest away."

Leaves are so thick there it is hard to tell day
From night and they say that shepherds never can
Tell the dusk hour from the beginning of dawn
If one would awaken after a very deep sleep,
Wondering what may have happened to his sheep.

John's Threat

John, eleven, declares to Evelyn, nine,
"Where is my white rabbit? Have you seen
My white rabbit any time this afternoon?"

"No," Evelyn replies, "I have not been
Near her cage; I have had my balloon
In front of the house playing with a friend of mine."

So it was I happened to overhear
The following typical threat that was childishly queer:

"If I could find one who knows where my rabbit is hid
I would open his head like cook opens up the lid
Of a tomato-can and I would look inside and see
Exactly where he knew my rabbit to be,

And if he acted like he wouldn't allow
It I believe I'd do it anyhow."

Revolution and the Sentries

They said nothing who had been taught to stand
Patiently by the door where all came in
And wait there all day with an outstretched hand,

They had forgotten how to frown and grin
And had something of the expression babies have
Whose facial muscles timidly await
The command of nerves whose development is late
And what is there is neither bold nor brave.

But those to whom no orders had been given at all
Laughed uproariously enough to split their cheeks,
They had not had, they claimed, so much fun in weeks

And when no one was coming down the hall
Each one looked at the other and said, "Well, well!
What do you think about it! What the hell!"

Now and Then

Courtesy was the predominant note
Struck by his metallic sideward glance
As he asked her if she wanted to dance.

She, aware of the cut of his dinner coat,
Answered yes as a planet might be told
By a curt Creator that it must not remain cold

But, charting its course now by a new set of logs,
Must leave its neighbors, nebulae and fogs
Of distant aether, and begin to take part
In a new universe very dear to the heart
Of the curt Creator who carefully planned such things

Just as he fixed the morning star so it sings
For fools like Donne and Blake to hear in their sleep
While early-birds hop about and earth-worms creep.

Two Friends Timider Than Most

I would say "Come in" but he would not come in,
My room was too warm, perhaps, or I had no chair
In which the wind could comfortably sit and be fair
To his own peculiar structure all the while.

No matter indeed, trees have almost the same style
Of paying calls, a neighboring pine tree below
Stands by my window ankle-deep in snow
And only taps when the wind makes too much din.

They are two friends that will never visit me
To sit them down to chat and drink my wine,

The wind, he only rattles on the door,
Whines a moment at its crack along the floor

Then rushes back to embrace the frigid pine
Outside my window who taps for me to see.

The Flies

Death came to him so quickly that the flies
In the room were unaware that he was dead,
Which is usually not the case.
                                    They avoided his head
Strangely enough and did not light on his eyes
At all as flies are very apt to do
When the blood stops to rest and the brittle ribs stop
        heaving
And the heat goes off while the last breath is leaving
And the work of the lungs and the brain is finally
        through.

They continued describing circles in the air
Using the light globe to describe a radius,

But toward dusk this must have become tedious
To them, judging from the deliberate care
With which they took it on themselves to stop
And rest for the night over the mantel-top.

Why He Stroked the Cats

He stroked the cats on account of a specific cause,
Namely, when he entered the house he felt
That the floor might split and the four walls suddenly
    melt
In strict accord with certain magic laws
That, it seemed, the carving over the front door meant,
Laws violated when men like himself stepped in,

But he had nothing to lose and nothing to win,
So in he always stepped. Before him went
Always his shadow. The sun was at his back.

The ceilings were high and the passageway was so black
That he welcomed the great cats who advanced to meet
    him
The two of them arching their soft high backs to greet
    him;

He would kneel and stroke them gently under their jaws,
All that is mentioned above being the cause.

Spotted Hides and Poor-grade Wool

There was a moon, a young one in the sky
And a cold breeze blowing from the upper air
And a rapid creek flowing not far from where
The salt lick was, where all the sheep were bedded
In the white moonlight one could see to read by
Were one a literary shepherd wedded
To printed pastorals instead of the natural ones
Ruled over by sun and moon and stars and seasons.

Shepherds that really cared about their sheep
Would never have left them out of doors to sleep
On such a night as this; they might be bewitched
And grow with spotted hides and poor-grade wool,

Valuable sheep always should be watched
And allowed to breed only when the moon is full.

Two Idle Dolphins over a Sunken Troop-Ship

One remarked, shifting a sharp black fin,
"This was a beautiful boat with its grey paint
And the brass that one time gleamed before the taint
Of salty water turned its gloss to green.

But where are the soldiers we could so plainly see
The times we leaped from the water to hear them shout
At the sight we made tumbling head-first out
To dive back heavily again into the sea?"

"They were here," replied the second one,
"Some days ago, but yesterday at dawn
A school of young sharks scuttled quickly past me
With guilty sideward glances;
                                        I could see
That they were not hungry from the disinterested way
They sniffed at food all the rest of the day."

You Can Never Tell

You can never tell what girls are going to do
Or what boys are thinking about. If you begin
By taking a pin and saying, "This is a pin,"
And hold it up where they can get a view

The girls are just as apt to leave the group
Particularly if they happen to be in love
Or the boys may remark "Look up above!
Watch that aviator loop the loop!"

If they happen to be outdoors talking together
And if it happens to be inclement weather
And the group is indoors listening to some one play
The sort of music not heard every day,

What may occur is unpredictable
And what does occur is quite incredible.

Warning to One

Death is the strongest of all living things
And when it happens do not look in the eyes
For a dead fire or a lack-lustre there,
But listen for the words that fall from lips
Or do not fall. Silence is not death;
It merely means that the one who is conserving breath
Is not concerned with tattle and small quips.

Watch the quick fingers and the way they move
During unguarded moments—words of love
And love's caresses may be cold as ice
And cold the glitter of engagement rings;
Death is the sword that hangs on a single hair,
And that thin tenuous hair is no more than love
And yours is the silly head it hangs above.

Parade

Yes, this must pass, this day and its parade
Of terrifying minutes tramping past
And others yet, for these are not the last.

Days are to be whose serried hours are laid
In fierce brigades across the fields of Time
Waiting the bugle note of circumstance
To give them all the signal to advance
And bring more nameless deeds than one could rhyme.

If you doubt me then look on the sun
Trailing his banner westward through the sky,

This breeze, no doubt, has blown in Araby,
And do you think that bird sings of fresh pain?

How many times, how many times again,
That cloud has fallen as rain on Babylon!

General Yes and Particular No

You who are ashes! What I most regret,
I who write, mainly on your account
And what you mean to me, I cannot forget
That though I can remodel all the font
Of what I will, I cannot put the water,
Holy, pure and brilliant, in the bowl
So that it will leap and flow and roll
Over the lips of those who wish for laughter
But have only tears that are too vainly shed
To ever recall the beauty that is dead
That once was yours.
                  I can recall with words
The house you dwelt in, even, and the birds
That flew over it in spring and in the fall,

But you I cannot ever recall at all.

After the Storm

But a great log had fallen across the road.

There was nothing for us to do but stop and wonder
How to get it away.
                        The rain and thunder
Were both about to end.
                              An invisible tree-toad
Was beginning to shrill the interrupted song
It had been singing earlier in the day
Before the clouds, that were now washed away
By the wind and rain, had ever come along
The paths in the sky that were especially prepared for
        them
By a Creator whose own name is dim
But whose bright deeds give all the universe light
From crimson planets sinking in their bed
And emerald clusters rising overhead
Of stars that populate the sunless night.

Her Largesse

The kingliest parts of him belonged to her.

He'd given them to her once when she was ill,
Lamely, perhaps, and somewhat against his will.

But now she held them closely like a fur
Robe about her when the winds beat snow
Against her figure that had far to go
Over a road over a hill so steep
Those who reached its end could only sleep;

His long square forehead and his long-lidded eyes,
She held them tightly as a jockey holds
The reins wrapped over his knuckles in double folds
When the wind has beaten his cap down in his face.
And this is perhaps the end of his last race
And to win it would be the key to paradise.

Stop the Parade

Stop the parade and let the feet be still
Between this valley and that distant hill.

Out of the East too long, too far they march
With steady tramp—tramp—tramp. The tongues will
  parch
And cleave to the roof of the mouth before they stop,
The bones will be dust, the blood will be earth again,
Pain will be pleasure and pleasure will be pain
Before they disappear over the dim hill-top.

Stop the parade—too long, too far already
The feet have tramped, the shoes are worn through and
  lost
And it is too great to count, the awful cost,
Soldier and gentleman, camp-follower and lady,

You have made your path too long that leads from the
  womb
In the dark back again through the light to the darkened
  tomb.

What the Winds Said to Adrian

⟦decorative border⟧

Adrian . . . Adrian . . . Adrian . . . (the voices
    lulled)
Your feet should not go treading where the fawns
Have cropped so closely to the bitter roots
Of the grass. You still march to the sound of lutes
And still unheeding, and you have seen many dawns
Through the vines from which the blooms were pulled
By those who danced so lightly in the sun
They forgot the intricate steps they had begun . . .

But rest you lightly now till Michaelmas,
Adrian, then we winds will come again
To you and sing to you our song for pain

While our voices blow to the east where shadows pass
After the orange sun has made his will
And is being interred by the clouds beneath a hill. . . .

The Longer I Watch

The longer I watch the heavens I see more stars
Until a certain hour, the break of dawn.

Naturally then of course they all are gone
But after the sun is set and I begin
To sweep the sky with tireless hungry eyes
In silent order one by one come in
Points of light, first slowly, then rapidly
Like guests arriving in a dim room for tea.

Then along midnight as Venus, Jupiter, Mars
And the jewels of the dippers swing across the skies

Strangers appear like famished animals
Whose eyes shine bright in the reflected fires
From the camp of the sun whose long processionals
Are halted underneath me to wait for day.

I Saw You First

I saw you first on a summer afternoon
Watering the lawn with a hose and a glittering jet
Of falling crystals shining in the sun.

On the shaded grass, drenched and soaking wet,
Neighbors might pass and you would answer their call
With a constant voice.
                         With that same voice I heard
You scold two puppies for romping too much with a ball
Or yapping under the locust tree at a bird.

Then Autumn descended out of her chariot of bronze,
Spring in her silver, Summer in her gold one had left,

And found your asters unready with rusted crowns,
And the puppies both half-grown dogs and you bereft
Of your olden voice, raking the fallen leaves
And snipping the moonflower vines that had grown to
     the eaves.

Pandora and the Moon

Minds awake in bodies that were asleep
Caused the winged troubles to be born
That made Pandora one time feel forlorn,

Because, in spite of the box, she could not keep
Her troubles there, the worrisome animalcules
Fluttered out never to be regained,
For every method of evil especially trained
And subject neither to God's nor the devil's rules.

What shall she do? Nothing, sit and ponder,
Watch the dying leaves drop from the tree
Until they all are gone and she may see
The same moon then that used to make her wonder
At the unbelievable stories she sits and reads,

And if she succeeds in that then she succeeds.

Mice in Sheaves

I know when no mice rustle in the sheaves
That Autumn is gone, that when the wind has whirled
The trees' high flags away that we call leaves
But are green banners that the frost has furled,
That Winter must follow and with it the sharp rain
And fierce snow from the clouds to besiege the earth
Till battle is over and singing return again
And then May's smile and April's open mirth.

But I hear no field-mice rustling in the sheaves
And the tall ash-tree has only tattered leaves
And the quail-calls are hushed, all that were ever given,

And the singing is gone and harvested the dreams
And I stay alone watching the evening heaven
Where birds are flying southward in thin streams.

IF I COULD SPEAK

If I Could Speak

If I could speak it would be for a zeal
 By which the hills are steep, the sea is deep,
By which sea-gulls sustain themselves in flight
And bright stars climb the fastnesses of night,

Zeal that bred and colored newt and eel,
Serpent and dragon, man and ant and flea,
The sweet arbutus and the acorn tree,
Zeal that penetrated Zephyr's mouth
To let a soft wind blow out of the south—

That glassy mountainside is hard and steep,
But borrow the zealous claws of the wolf to climb,
It is cold there even in the day-time
On those heights that zeal will take you to—
But borrow the wolf's coat, do what the wolf would do.

Too Large by Day, Too Small by Night for Us

The world by day is enormous. We are tiny
Spots that dot the turf or at times the briny
Sea with our swimming pates; we are small specks
That pollute the air from which we break our necks
As we fall in flaming planes. We are the robe
Of born and dying mortals that contains
All that is left of Erda's poor remains;
By day the world is large, untimorous.

But at night the world shrinks down, decreases size;
It becomes a circle of light around a fire,
A halo around a candle or a globe.
Outside lies fear, the dark and ominous
Unknown, the large, the danger, the monstrous
Image craven and the visage dire.

"S.S. Carobel"

Ships cost dollars, pounds, marks, lire, francs,
And weigh stone, tons and kilos, sail knots, miles,
Between the coasts of countries, sink, burn, rust,
Wear out, are bought, sold, lost, and carry men
To and from the hearts of waiting women,
Elicit at the dock cheers, tears and smiles,
Obey the waves' whim, follow the winds' pranks,
By surge and tide and swell are rocked and tossed

But is it not unbelievable and strange
How now this faëry vessel can depart
Out of such haven for a distant mart
Skimming and cleaving so miraculously
The foamy meadows of the noisy sea,
Is it not unbelievable and strange?

You Tell Me Morning

Now, if dawn were no more than what you smile
At me—still it would dawn and morning sun
Would rise as easily as both your eyes
Unlid themselves as you look up at me
Unmercifully and yet compassionately,

It would still dawn and sunrise all the while
You hold me in the chambers of your eyes,

It would still day—you are the only one
To make such miracle without surprise,
To make such miracle and then apprise
Me quickly of its making with your eyes

That rise deep-lidded, greet me with a stare
To tell me sun and morning are both there,
I who alone would never be so wise.

Yes, You Might as Well

You might as well be ready now as ever
To accept the gift of which Time is the giver
Par excellence—and you may call this prose
And smile and say, "I wonder if this man knows
That what he is saying has been said before
And better by better men." Yes. One time more
However I cry, "Mortality, you are Man."
Which was old before you started or I began
To look over printed pages with curious eyes,
And say, "This one is a fool—that one is wise,"
Critically, ephemerally, until
You are the man shot dead across the sill
Of the door to the house of life you thought was yours
Until another tenant made it his.

Sleepy Water

Have you ever slept—slept like a water-fall
Falling somewhere over a stony ledge
Into a pool of slumber far below—?

Have you ever fallen in sleep, fallen below
The margin of this world, below its edge
Into something nebulous and slow
Like the Milky Way of sleep? Did you ever fall
Insistent, ceaseless, like a water fall
Over the bed you slept on—did you drop
Into the Gulf Stream of sleep and never stop
Sinking, dissolving into sleep—did you
Ever do what I'm trying to tell you to
Do—drop—fall—sink—slip away—dissolve
Into the water of sleep, the water of sleep?

Birds on the Wire

How simple mathematics is applied!
How happy, helpful, fortunate it is!

One is a number, millions are mysteries;
1 is I, x is the race of Man
That dignifies itself with lust and pride
And has continued so since time began
Progressing along strict mathematical lines
From Past through Now to what the Future divines.

And letters! See the orderly alphabet,
A B C, and so on, like birds on a wire!

And they fly up and settle down again, but yet
No water nor flame has quelled their heat and fire;
All the words in the world out of twenty-six
Letters for us to re-arrange and fix.

Night Is Filled With

The sleepless aged or their weary dreams,
Their shrivelled hands and shrunken-lidded eyes,
Silent vigils through the lonely night,
The howling wind and footsteps in the dark,
The rafter-creak, the cock-crow or the bark
Of a distant dog, the murmur of green leaves
Or faces peering into the still air
Through blank windows, the thin flame that weaves
Shadow-carpets by the street-lamp's glare,
The monotone repeated by the streams
On hidden gravel-beds, the tremulous wise
Cold cries of owls, the scampering in fright
Of mice across dry attics, dusty floors,
The screeching hinge and the bang of wind-closed doors.

O Mad Spring, One Waits

O mad spring that taught the silent grass
To die for winter, spring that taught the sun
Its quick commandments, winds of spring that run
Before the months of summer, O mad spring
That forces icicle and frost to pass,
That taught the savage trees to stand and call
With a green cry that echoes until fall,

Spring that does not heed the signalling
Colors of my desire, O spring, one waits
And envies seasons and their certain fates,
Drawing pitiless and tiring breath,
Watching shadows from the sun of death
Darken as its light pales, one still stands
Pressed by fear and hunger on both hands.

For the Strange Children

Have you food for your hunger? Are there shoes
On your feet? A shelter over your head?
When you are weary do you have a bed
To go to? Is there a fire in your house?
Lonely? Another heart to unburden with,
Another one to tread the silent path
Leading from yesterday into tomorrow
Lined with grass of grief and trees of sorrow?

Then you do not need what I would give
If you have all—I sing for the lonely ones,
Brave fingers cut by thorns, feet bruised by stones
Whose salvage is the fragments they would save
Out of the gathering wrecks that strew this shore,
This strange cold strand they never saw before.

Memory

Memory is a warm bath that dissolves
The scabs of pain and hunger from the mind.

Memory lets the past be pleasant and
Memory lets the unhappy soul be blind
To evils that have walked abroad the land.

Memory, after the hunt, gives to the selves
Their equal portions of the fickle quarry
That Hand or Face have captured.
                                              Memory
Never lets the consciousness miscarry
What is due as duty to Memory.

Memory, when happy, is the last
Part of the person to dread turning sorry.

Memory is the path that you may take
To see the living unborn, the dead awake.

The Story of Vivauno

When he was young the satyrs came and stole
Him from his duty shepherding fat sheep
And took him to a grotto where a sleep
Fell on him. And there he slept the whole
Winter through and never dreamed or waked
Except for thirst that never had been slaked
For white and purple wine in the oak casks
Filled by the satyrs as their yearly tasks;

He waked and drank the wine, then slept again
How many days he did not know but when
He rose and thought at last he could not tell
How much time had passed or what befell
Him in that grotto where there only were
Emptiness and shadow and thin air.

Attributes of the Night Sky

Night is a hill that not only the stars
Climb to a zenith then descend with awe;

We too answer that impervious law
To praying, tears and laughter; we obey
That code of alternates, night versus day,

We too ascend to midnight then to dawn
Descend before the last pale star is gone
Or withered behind the glowing sunrise bars.

We climb the hill of night; its crest is not
Exactly on the twelve but nearer three
O'clock. Then are children born and on the sea
Ships go down and nothing marks the spot;
Silently the dying die, then even
Space and Time do not pertain to heaven.

Fish at Night

The way fish swim in a phosphorescent sea
Viewed from the prow of a boat has now become
So much a wonder that it cannot be
Very far from the millennium
Of wonders; jasper, onyx, obsidian,
None are as dark and hard, as cold and smooth
As is the water's surface except where waves
Swell and dash and break against the prow
That cuts the water like a plow and shaves
The surface of its foam.
                              Deep in it now
Dart swift fish like magic—and in truth
No tongue could tell how swift, with what disdain
They dart away and outward from the prow
As it comes near, no prophet could tell how.

Mother Earth

You are a strange mother, Mother Earth:
Never failing when your children call
Yet never heeding when they cry at all,
O paradoxical mother!
                    If a dearth
Would fall on them it would be out of you,
Yet is never annalled what you do
Though in the midst of immanent new crises
You never cease to shower with surprises
Out of your lap your children that petition
Help and forgiveness.
                  Loyalty, sedition,
All are equal, both are ever the same
That you produce to carry and tread on your name;

You have produced us all and will receive
Us all on a day we do not dare to grieve.

Man with a Burden

That name will not be borne away by wind.
Whatever his burden is wind cannot blow
It from his shoulders; he must rise and go
As men have always gone in the rough wind
That tears from some men many useless vestures
But never this one's attitudes and gestures.

The wind can never tear away the fame
That is his special burden; the long name,
Futile denomination, fearsome nomenclature
Of destiny that is his destiny:

The wind may mutter tremolo and whinny
Persuasively—the burden will not fall.

O fardel! From what source derives your nature
That is this man's full nothing, empty all?

Monotonous, the Needless Endless Words

He said the words, no more. He only said
The words. They flowed like water from a tank
Or cistern of rain water that had stood
A long time since its filling and grown stale,
Flat like warm rain water in a pail.

He said the words; no one would ever quail,
Obey or fear his orders—no one shrank
Or leaped to execute what he had bid;

He said the words. They flowed like rotten water
Out of a tepid vessel: not one sad
Or joyous grimace helped them—not one mad
Gesture or quick beckon helped the water
His words were flowing. Now, is there then no
End to these dull words that come and go?

Something: Man

There is something about a man that makes
A woman attentive when his voice speaks,

Something about a man makes a woman stop,
Survey his figure from the foot to top,
Cap-a-pie. There is something about a man
That melts the crystals of the coldest woman:
Diamonds by moonlight—they are she—
That fuse in his fire of masculinity.

Femininity is no and man is yes,
Man is go, woman is always stay,
Man tomorrow, woman is yesterday,
Man is a fact and woman is a guess;

Let the woman negate the world who can
Or deny the positivity of a man.

Something: Woman

Something about a woman makes a man
Stop, become aware, look and listen.

Men dissolve in air but crystallize
Out of solution when a woman's eyes
Focus on them. When a woman turns
And looks at a man a fraction of him dies
That should not have been born; the lonely beast
Starves for lack of food on which to feast.

He sees the cup filled ready for him to drink,
He sees the thought formed ready for him to think,
In his head there is a light that burns
Brighter and shines out under his eyelids

When a woman stares at him and sees
More than many speechless mysteries.

Dawn Thoughts Before a Busy Day

Somewhere a clock was striking, indicating
The passage of time—what was time? He had never
Seen time though he had heard of its spell
That bloomed men out and dried them up until
Their bodies were wisps to blow to heaven or hell
According to the wind—was time the wind?
Wind that could be felt as well by the blind
Who could not see it as by the well that could?

And was there any purpose now in stating
If ever there was, whether evil or good
The passage of time turned out to be or how
Time passed the past, turned it into the now,
The now into the future and so on—
Somewhere a clock was striking. It was dawn.

Where Are the Days of Seeking Now

The days that so austere attended us
Upon our imminent search that yielded nought,
Where are they now that stood like sentinels
Over our path? Suns dawned, suns sank, and they
Ushered the day out, ushered in the day
Ominously, officially, and we,
Staid and sedate, walked by them as the bells
Of high search pealed importantly somewhere
And broke their music in the crystal air
To scatter it benignly on our heads.

Where are they now, those days through which we
        fought
Seriously, preserving patiently
Our efforts that perhaps a trove tremendous
As our searching would reward our deeds?

Genii Loci, the Spirits of the Place

There is no great unfitness that the pearls
Of life should be cast down before the swine
Of death. Whoever stubbornly declares
That dust is an unjust and lawless end
For all, is wrong and only to defend
This hope I offer signs, slight slender signs
As difficult as the flavor in rare wines
To detect—signs difficult to name,

That lurk in the dress of nature and the same
In the gear of earth, and in the noise
Made in their play by the celestial boys,
Heard in the voices of the fairy girls
That live in trees and rocks, and in the whine
Of comets, shooting stars and meteors.

Now with Colors Far too Fanciful

Now with colors far too fanciful
The aged autumn trees are decked and draped.

A volleying wind but recently has scraped
The sky of summer tint and in the lull
That follows autumn's slow inauguration
Messages from winter are received:

The latest trees must be at last unleaved,
That is the worst, most final proclamation
That issues from cool cylinders of clouds
Above our eyes, eyes that are turned to heaven.

Soon will winter with more somber dyes
Change the shades of hill and meadow even
To a still duller hue than the raw clods
That fill the soil's uncharted vacancies.

City Lunch Hour

Toward noon the hot sun baked the pavement brown
In the red, weary city. Buildings rose
By thousands into the air like strange steel trees—
Weird forests of stone by daylight—and men ran
And shouted in all directions, even those
Who would walk or be silent, even these
Who would not so, and motors rumbled by
Jarring the earth and shaking the warm sky.

In a terse moment Jack went into the street,
Crossed a corner, stopped a pause and breathed
And watched a face the sunlight had just wreathed
With a yellow glow, then as a thousand feet
Trampled by, not without perceptible shock,
He went in a store and bought a dollar alarm clock.

Village Noon: Mid-day Bells

When both hands of the town clock stood at twelve
Eve ceased spinning, Adam ceased to delve.

A lusty cockerel crowed that noon had come,
The shadows stood beneath the trees and some
Were motionless a moment—then the people
Busied themselves for food and in the steeple
Ubiquitous pigeons roucoulayed and slept
Above the watch the dogs below them kept
For nothing—or a dust cloud down the road
That might mean feet or might mean wheels or not.

Then as the noon sun with its ardor glowed
On man and beast and field and dwelling place
The hands moved past noon to another spot
And Time moved on a little way in Space.

ACIDS, BASES AND SALTS

Poet

Why do you, whenever you are addressed,
Dash your brains out, sir, all over the floor?
Against the wall or against an open door
As if you suddenly felt that you were pressed
By impolite circumstance to act that way?

Are you not aware that if you were dead
Hordes of swallows would still fly overhead
Twittering while they blackened the unfortunate day
That you have not yet decided may have to occur
Without your intervention while you dream
In blackened gardens where white peacocks scream
And you are dust that cannot interfere
With others, who perhaps like you will insist on crushing
Their fragile skulls out of which their brains come
    rushing?

Young Men

Why is it that young men never succeed?

Various reasons, voices behind the stars
Whisper against them while comets sent as spies
Burn and blind the chambers of their eyes
With bright comet-tails and glowing comet-dust;

Then, outside of that I know there must
Be other reasons why they are put behind bars
And given only the meagerest food they need,

Other reasons we can never know,
Inscrutable causes, possibly arteries and veins
That fail to nourish properly young men's brains
So that the cells there wholly fail to grow
And let them know that voices back of the stars
Are not enough to keep them behind bars.

Carrion

If it should ever be correctly determined
How the Cyclops came to have only one eye,

Then let the ones whose cause it has been to cry
Their own foolish story about it to men who are ermined
And maced and throned and armed with scepter and
    crown,

Let those absurd ones be given time enough
To see their condition grossly and in the rough
And then be shown water deep enough to drown
Their lugubrious bodies in, that have long been cadaver-
    ous
But so well perfumed and attired that it could not be
    told,

For if they do not, when they grow really old,
Vultures and crows who are very hard to fool
May come and seize them, screaming and mutinous,
And carry them off without writ or protocol.

Acquiescence to Universal Reality

They would accept the flesh but cannot trust it,
It having been known to decay so many times
As poets have told in thousands of feet of rhymes
Feeble as this, lamenting the fall of the rose,
The soot on the snow, the taint of brine in the sea,
The smirching of the lily, the down-cut tree,
The crumbled house, the wall with a gap in it,
The sunken ship, the cloud dissipated by wind,
The speck in ointment, the flaw in the crystal heaven,
The key without a lock, the lock without a key,
The soured wine, the bread baked without leaven,
The meat defiled, killed by one who sinned,
The paradise where the fruit of all knowledge grows
To be eaten by others but not by you and me.

Fire

Call the fire engines out! Turn the hydrants on!
Unhook the chemical carts! Let the water run!

Because a heart is burning in that house
Though it is as quiet as a mouse
And though the blinds are all drawn tightly shut.

Do not ponder now that the cause is what
You think the cause to be, but scream alarm
So that he can hear it whose hand and arm
Set fire to the heart that burns within!

He who has no cognizance of his sin
And will only greet with apathetic stare
The earth and sea and sky, the land and air,
And watch a butterfly glitter as it flits
About in the gutter where everybody spits.

On the Grand Tour 1638-1639

Milton said, I saw the golden chain
Almost with my own eyes but not quite,
I could see it far off and the light
With which it glowed penetrated my brain,
It held the earth suspended in chaos there
Out of hell's reach, attached to heaven's floor,
That was after the mutinous angels had fallen down
From Peter's village to Lucifer's teeming town.

Galileo answered, Yes, so Ptolemy thought.
For one of his day he knew as much as he ought.
I feel that the sun no longer circles us
If it ever did—it's not that generous,
We move about it and as to where the rain
Spills from I don't know nor the golden chain.

Ratiocinatio Religiosi

If you need the words ask for them
And they will fall to you straight from Jesse's lips
Or open the Book to any page by chance
And there before you (marvellous circumstance)
You will find the wind that other ships
Than yours have blessed for wafting to quiet water,

Or go to a room where the atmosphere is stiller
Than where you work, where the air is dim,
And touch whatever you will there with your hand,

Whatever it is, read it and understand
That the everlasting mercy is everlasting
And yours to share no matter how devastating
Are the brutal days that advance armed with sharp
    spears
And keen-edged swords against the heart that fears.

Books and Men

Millions of people talking about other people
In book-shop talk and literary reviews,
Passing gossip, criticism, trade-news

Like church organs whose chimes are set in the steeple
To scatter down when crowds congregate within
The battle cries of unknown soldiers lost
In wars lamenting the ultimate gain and cost
Of whether the right were good and the evil were sin
And who did just what thing in just what way,

Millions of people talking about themselves
In millions of volumes dusty on millions of shelves

And everywhere dust, settling down and grey
On faces that might have shown white in the bright
    moonlight
Somewhere once, perhaps on a certain night.

Harvest

Smoke your pipe, sir, — smoke your grey pipe,
Smoke your pipe till its rings surround the moon
And make of the moon a Saturn, it will be soon
When all shall know that your head will never be ripe
For plucking into a basket along with the others
That are early or late ripe as the case may be
And are already plucked or shaken off the tree,
They that started out to be your brothers.

Smoke your pipe. Grind the tobacco in your fist,
Look over your glasses as if you knew it all,

You who know nothing, no, you do not know the call
By which wild geese commune, the last with the first,
Over dead waters and sterile prairie lands
Where hunters wander, shot-guns in their hands.

The Ruby Flood

Though ink evaporates and wears away
Words that are written in blood will never fade
But will last as long as the tough paper will last
That holds them there together.
                              Let the day
That will be unable then to decipher the code
That we write in take heed at what has passed
In cities that dry and rot now in the sun,
Pergamum, Krokodilopolis, Babylon.

For all they need to note is that the word
Their eye beholds is written in red blood
Turned black by time, for surely they have heard
Of the wasteful way that silly lovers have
Of borrowing penfuls of the ruby flood
Flowing from their heart, to be known beyond the grave.

Answers Are in the Back of the Book

This is the reason that we have so little
Now that so many others have so much:

It was agreed by the ultimate factors who
Determine that cats shall mew and lions shall roar
That we be accorded only this jot and tittle
We have and not one item for subtraction

For if it were not so, answers might not be true
In the everlasting text-book of addition

And it might be said by loose-tongued angels or devils,
"God does not figure correctly as he should."

Or, "That is only one of the several evils
That twists the straightness of the heavenly Good
That is supposed to be projected as a straight line
From one point, God's heart, to another point, mine."

Arbor Vitae

Plato himself knew what most men now know
About this round globe that we live upon,

And about its clients the stars and its patron the sun
And its dead relatives covered with aether and snow
That slowly spin down the oblivious years
To planet grave-yards whence no sphere returns
No matter how its obdurate center burns
To rotate and whirl along with the other spheres.

And there are men, the Platos of today,
Who scan printed pages with spectacled eyes
To vision there an eugenic paradise

Where neither too much work exists nor play
And all men are just what each one should be;
Proper leaves and roots nourishing the tree.

Man Who Could Not Tell When It Was Going to Rain

When it was going to rain did he look at the sky
And remark, "It's getting hazy over there."

"The sun's still shining but I rather fear
We're due a lot of rain this time of the year."

"Although today is warm and the weather's fair
The clouds are massing, they're not riding high
And passing over as they do when it's going to be dry."

"I think I'd better go back into the house and try
To find my new umbrella, the one of silk."

No, friend, no, ah, no, he would not do that;
Out he would dash, wearing his best suit and hat,
Cleaned and pressed, he would not look at the sky,

He'd jabber, "Will it rain today, it's very dry?"
And later a rain-storm would break and clabber the
    milk.

The Story the Idiot Tried to Tell

Nevertheless, one who claims such things
Must have recourse to lamps or wishing rings
That bring with a rush out of spaces behind the moon

Gifts that we should never possess so soon
That we forget their nature and the cause
Of our having them and how many unworded laws
Had to work together to bring them to us
From the immemorial home of the incubus
And the succubus adolescents dream about
When lessons are over and classes are turned out,

The monster that often lurks in groves of trees,
Who never mentions any of the things he sees
And if accosted by courageous souls
Turns into dew and filters down worm-holes.

On the Development of Certain Personalities

People like that develop much as sea-shells
Of curious shapes slowly come into being,
So slowly there is never any seeing
How it is done, but a slight incident tells
How much they are different, if you knew them before
Particularly,
              once, for example, they were thus:
A single whorl or two, no nucleus,
But now they are elaborate monstrosities
Small and unrecognizable except at the core
Which is invisible.
              He only sees
Who remembers stage by stage how they became,
From namable forms, forms without a name,

Now ground by the ocean against an unending shore
To become the same particles they once were before.

Overhead in a Family Mausoleum

Those who had been beautiful never could bring them-
    selves
To admit that they were no longer so as they lay
Carefully sealed in lead from the light of day,
Silently dark in vaults on burial shelves,

But those who had been hideous in every way they knew
Were able to smile and remark, "Perhaps it's true
That we who were second missed nothing by not being
    first
And what we are through with may be considered the
    worst
Without admitting that Life is an empty pan
A fool beats on with a bone and if he can
Dents through,
                    and if anyone lives who feels
That it is not Time but innate Death that steals
The teeth away from the gums and the hair from the
    head
Then so might he, just as we all, be dead."

Liquids

Liquids we use have always seemed to me
Stranger even than what we use them for,

Ink is an instance, uncork it with care,
It is astounding when you suddenly see
Words formed of it spread on an empty page
That was only paper before it met the ink
And to know that from it unborn men may drink
The sweet or bitter thought of a perished age.

One may consider, though one may forget,
Mysterious humours of the most daily kind;

Milk, out of which the shapes of our bones are laid,
Or drugs that cut the cords in Memory's net
Allowing the fish-like thoughts to escape and hide
In the thin streams that trickle through the mind.

Fear Analysis

Reduce your fears in an ultimate analysis, sir.
What do they equal then?
                              Answer me that
In as careful terms as with which you buy your hat
Or select a necktie out of seventeen more

And what now camps in the valleys of your brain
Will put out its fire and slip away and you
Who it seems have never known just what to do
Will look in your mirror and find that you are sane.

Boil your fears in hot acids in your mind,
Bake them with alkalies, grind them with coarse earth,

Dissolve, distill what is left; you will have a dearth
Instead of the old plenty but you will find
That the residue steeped in water makes a drink
That is pleasant to sip when one must sit and think.

Waiting for the Earth to Cool

The first time I came the earth was a liquid globe
Of fire whirling somewhere out in space
That glowed so fiercely I had to turn my face
Away, there was not any protecting robe
Of misty clouds above to help keep me cool;

So I went back to where I had been before
And said, "I'll wait a million years or more,"
Which I did, "Until that nebula-like pool
Of burning star-dust cools enough for me
To rest a while there as I have always planned."

I came again and found the forests spanned
With fabulous monsters that hung from tree to tree,

That meant another wait, so I went away
And now return; this time I think I will stay.

The Book of How

After the stars were all hung separately out
For mortal eyes to see that care to look
The one who did it sat down and wrote a book
On how he did it.
                    It took him about
As long to write the book as to do the deed
But he said, "It's things like this we mostly need."
And the angels approved but the devils screamed with
        laughter
For they knew exactly what would follow after.

For somehow he managed entirely to omit
The most important facts in accomplishing it,

Where he got the ladder to reach the stars
And how he lighted them, especially Mars,

And what he hung them on when he got them there
Eternally distant and luminous in the air.

Scientia Vincit Omnia?

Salts were formed by acids combined with bases
Under proper conditions, that was easy to see.

He was acid, also easy, but she . . .
A weak base only to be used in certain cases
To unite with an acid that was rather weak?

He was not sure. It seemed as though she was
But he was never sure of it because
He never could quite bring himself to speak.

So laboratory—laboratory—laboratory—
On it went, three days out of six,
Chemicals here, chemicals there,—do they mix?

The ancient characters acting the ancient story,
And just as sure as young birds learn to sing,
Love in a test-tube he knew was a dangerous thing.

Men Have Died

Men have died—worms have eaten them
But not for love? Swear that this is true
And all the birds that are fated to be blue
By reasons known only to God's secretary
Will bring dead leaves and help us both to bury
The overgrown grief that lost its diadem
And its mace and even its royal signet ring
The moment its throne crumbled and the thing
That caused all this to happen took its place.

Without a doubt the color on your face
Means merely that this may or may not be true?

Nevertheless, all I say to you
I mean, for I know that ultimately Death
Will come and steal away even my own breath.

Daemons into Aether and Dragons into the Sea

He was their dream but he has been bought and sold
So many times that the patina is lost
And now is tarnished in spite of the first cost
That gilded him with gold that was more than gold,
More than the dazzling metal that men seek
In all the mountains and valleys of the earth.

So many hours have passed now since his birth
From the original source, that he is weak
And has not now the charm that anciently
Drove daemons into aether and dragons into the sea
Before his bitter force and subtle strength.

Now he is battered and tired and lies at length
Prone in the dust of the crowded market place
And dares let no man look upon his face.

The Poet Tells About Nature

What if the winds sang softly the whole night long
On the wet beach wandering slowly up and down,

What if the winds there sang so loud a song
That the waves were hushed, waves that were loud and
     strong
And older than the wind, waves stronger grown
Being closer to earth.
                    Winds might swing over a town
But the face of the earth the waves would finger long
After the winds were asleep and the sun was down.

What if the winds and the waves sung? I cannot tell you
Other than that they both themselves once lulled me
To sleep in the sea-grass beside a cold salt sea

Under a sky that was brilliant with stars and blue
With the justifiable expectation of dawn
For the sun was a long time set and its glow was gone.

Unending, Ceaseless, Interminable

When the last debt is paid and the last
Obligation fulfilled and the last
Duty executed and the last
Promise is complied with and the last
Wish is accomplished as well as the last intention,

When everything is done that one can mention
And all is arranged and in order and nothing remains
To be attended to by hands or solved by brains,

Then, only then, you are ready to begin.

Out of your loins flow seeds that cry for more
Life, work, wealth, love and trouble,

Men and women, they may meet with double
What you know; win all there is to win,
For the next generation it all remains and more.

The Noise That Time Makes

The noise that Time makes in passing by
Is very slight but even you can hear it,
Having not necessarily to be near it,
Needing only the slightest will to try:

Hold the receiver of a telephone
To your ear when no one is talking on the line
And what may at first sound to you like the whine
Of wind over distant wires is Time's own
Garments brushing against a windy cloud.

That same noise again but not so well
May be heard by taking a small cockle-shell
From the sand and holding it against your head;

Then you can hear Time's footsteps as they pass
Over the earth brushing the eternal grass.

SEEING

Alexander, Caesar, Napoleon

Ridiculous names, adorning dull façades
Of futile public buildings—you cannot be
More decayed or dead than you today
Are.
      What contribution did you give
That has not fallen as water through the sieve
Of our necessity?
                You cannot keep step
With acute emergencies that drop
Out of massing clouds in the east sky.

You are outspaced, outdistanced far too far
In time's geography to be any more
Than what you are, still images, trite words,

Shattered vehicles and rusty swords
On the junk-heap of mortality
Waiting a moment to be hauled away.

Office Assistant that got on My Nerves

He had the damnedest and most irritating
Way of talking, of reading telegrams
To me. He was always getting himself in jams
And coming to me to see if I were able
To get him out;—he jittered always, always,
On Sundays just as badly as on week-days,
And he always took rapid steps or quick short steps,
And his hands always fluttered and always tiny drops
Of perspiration stood on his forehead
And occasionally, when he sneezed hard, his nose bled.

As office assistant I have never had
So trying, tiring a person to work with,
And yet his manners were meant to be the breath
Of courtesy and deference and control!

City Traffic in the Auto Age

Motors leap like jaguars in the traffic
With the quick decision steel has got,
While the walking and the driving public
Lets its muscles move on reflex thought.

Lights change: ruby subterranean
Turns the vivid glint of iceberg's green,
Or changes yellow as the sunlight's glare,

While down the streets of the metropolis
And up them go processions that histories
Of other planets never saw before.

Headlights blink and glow and fenders stare
Silent an instant, vibrating the air
From their mudless polish, mirroring back
The quiet houses by the mobile track.

Aged Dowager Standing in Sunlight

The stone wall did not warm the old woman's hands:
The fact that her name was known in many lands
Did not warm her, either; she was cold.

Though sunlight turned the masonry to gold
She stood by, it was a windbreak, that was all;
An aged woman stood against a wall.

Her thoughts went musing much like honey-bees
Over flowers; here were some of them:

My daughters are harlots, I am growing dim,

I am as old as Newton and gravity;

Now I know what means the odour from the dead—

The corpse of a human contains within its smell
The scent of everything in the world that fell
As apples from Time's tree upon God's head.

A Corner for Letty

Letty was always miserable and dejected,
Nervous, lonely, grubby, and neglected.

As an infant she was always dirty and wet;
If a child fretted, she was the one to fret.

It was Letty who snivelled and Letty who picked her
    nose,
She was no lily—Letty was never a rose.

In children's games the others were bold and pretty
In drawing up sides, but no one ever chose Letty.

Later it was just the same, if it was not worse:
Through no fault of Letty's, Time chose not to disburse
Any store of good fortune that might have been allotted
    to her,
And Letty was avoided when all the others were
Mating and picking the fields for their serious work.
All Letty got was a corner in which to lurk.

Joseph Lauren

"God has always been neighbor to me, God
Companied me when I spoke and where I went,
Though not on sorrow often I was bent
But much more and usually on mirth."

But Lauren was also lonely as he strode,
Whether he was walking, whether he rode,
On frequent evenings through the shuttered streets,
Passing lighted windows, fascinated
With all he knew not that might be occurring
There to the people in their multiple lives.

Yet he married and outlived three wives
And died at ninety-seven, a fitful man
Packed with fire and quaintness as he was,
Himself his beacon and himself his cause.

The Bloody Auction Sale and She Was There

Something definitely terrible
About the auctioneer, about the people
Who came to buy, upset, electrified
The silence of the room. They, listening,
Watched . . . His hammer strokes began to ring.
In a voice modulous with pride
He cried the articles, he told the story
Of each; blood spattered, and the room was gory.

They bought her bed, her chair, her books, her lamp,
—The walls oozed blood, with blood the rug was
        damp—
Her shoes, even dresses on hangers, and her table
Were sold, recorded, quick as he was able:

Something absolutely horrible
Surrounded him and her and all the people.

Mr. Davenport's Will is Ignored

No hunting, trapping, or trespassing signs,
Upon his land, the owner Davenport
Erects, that all who take or kill in sport
Go otherwheres or alter their designs.

But beasts and birds that read no human words
Continue to come there, devour and prey
Upon each other singly and in hordes
And hunt or kill and eat or let decay . . .

And so with mortals from the city near:
Small boys come there a-trapping—lovers, too,
In pairs trespassing when the nights are clear
Do what lovers there are wont to do—

So it is now, so will it be the day
When Mr. Davenport is passed away.

The Difference Between Them Was Always Ample

None of the clocks in Pemberton's house ever
Told the correct time at a given hour.

Take four o'clock in the afternoon, for example:
One might say ten minutes, another a quarter, to four,
And like as not the one in the kitchen would say
Five or ten or fifteen minutes after four.

His clocks were a good deal like him, Samuel,
Who was never on time for anything in his life,
Though he spent a large part of it collecting clocks
And winding them and taking them apart
And putting them back together inaccurately;

Even though he wasted most of his life
Inviting silly people in to tea
To see his clocks and his goiterous French wife.

The Prince of Wales

My admiration for the Prince of Wales
Is far-flung as a fleet of royal sails.

Poor fellow, duties he must do as prince,
Endless, fatiguing, and yet never wince!

The clothes, the uniforms he has to wear
And shave his face and brush his British hair!

The letters he receives and telegrams
To be answered outweigh several Buckinghams!

The gentle dignity he must preserve,
Yet not lack tact or thought or wit or verve!

What he must sponsor, where officiate,
Events witness, documents dictate . . .

As deep as cotton in a thousand bales
My sympathy is for the Prince of Wales!

Me?

—Is that me, Monsieur Miroir, is that man
With a dusky face, with a deep coat of tan
From something, but not this earth's sun, around the
    eyes,
Staring out of my looking-glass in surprise—
Is that me, Monsieur Miroir, is he me?

—Yes, so far as I know, insofar as
I can tell it is you or it is what was
You one time, or it is what yet remains
Of one whose spirit died and the remains
Went on going where your body is.

—Why, then, Monsieur Miroir, do I walk
As if I had no breath or words to talk?
Why, then Monsieur Miroir, do I seem
As if I were or waked not from a dream?

Sweet Cheat Gone

Here is the living-room where Androcles
Spent his mornings, here the window-seat
Where Androcles watched passers in the street.

Here is the stairway and here is the hall
Where he walked and climbed, if he did at all.

Here is the table where his lunch was set
And here is the bed where Androcles would forget
Us all in sleep; here is the chair, the lamp,
Where Androcles read of evenings.
                             Androcles
Rarely ventured out beneath the trees
In his park behind his rugged wall.
Androcles never went for drives at all.
Androcles lived here one time, Androcles died
Life-spent roofs beneath and walls inside.

They Also Stand . . .

At midnight, in the garden never planted,
They are unwanted, they were never wanted.

The wanderers in the dark have never come
Upon their use and uses in the kingdom—
The garden with so many in daylight,
With the sun to paint their faces white,
Who were wanted, who were always wanted.

Always asking permission to stand there,
Begging the heel of a loaf, something to wear,
Asking for faggots, fuel, asking for food
(They had none of any), all of them stood,
Standing there as if they were rooted there
Begging, and whether it is fair or unfair,
I, standing apart, have seen them standing there.

Unknown White Man in the City Morgue

Tortured body, lie at rest alone
Finally on the long and merciless
Slab of now cool lava-molten stone
And wait our mutual and ending guess
At your identity, nameless, homeless one.

On suburb avenue, no numbered house
We know for you; no date of birth or death
Are yours, though somewhere visitors may carouse
In a domicile where you once lived,
Fathered, sonned and brothered, lovered, wived.

But now you come unfollowed to this place—
With an anonymous grimace on your face
In death—whose last name and whose last address
Will be yours in your latest loneliness.

Esquire

But you see many more days on ahead—
Do you not, sir?—long days of derby hats,
Suspenders, belts and taxicabs and spats,
Moronic clubs and vile untasting beer,
And mornings whose approach you hate and fear,
And hours when you are fed and fed and fed
With what, for what, by what (why hell!) and still
Neither the silence nor the noises kill.

Gone are the days—dismembered the bright shape
That new moons used to bring and the new grape,

Warm summer nights and happy, laughing crowds
Of young eyes. In the distance do you see,

Do you not see, sir, sunsets and the clouds
Banking them high in chastened memory?

John Arnold

I saw you once, John Arnold, as you were
Polishing what remained of the Morning Star,
After it was forgot by William Blake
And withered. You were polishing it to take
It out of heaven to hang in your own room
Perhaps—and once I looked in your poor room.

You were there alone, John Arnold, in the dust,
And damp and spider-webs and iron-rust
That had accumulated in its gloom.

And I saw you once, John Arnold, when you heard
Stranger music than the throat of a bird
Ever made; then your face was drawn and thin
And long and tired; you had walked to where
The winds of winter swept the glacial air.

The Magic Blacksmith

In a village where I lived a year
Was the kind of blacksmith Wagner wrote about.

They said his forge fires never had gone out
And, as his face was rather sinister,
He was the sort of a man a girl would fear.

He knew a lot; both his hands were stout,
He could twist an iron horse-shoe inside out
To please small boys if some were standing near.

One time I watched him when no one else was there;
It was supper-time and the Evening Star
Had just appeared. I said, "I wish there were more."

"So!" he answered almost in a shout;
Then he seized the red-hot end of an iron bar
And hammered it till white stars filled the air.

Hunter, Hunter, and the Fleeting Hind

Wherever Rodrigo goes by night, by day,
He sees the Hind and frightens it away.

Into the world Rodrigo goes; he sees
The White Hind frequently among the trees.

By the sea, along the yellow strand,
He sees the Hind a-snuffing at the sand.

By volcanoes, beside the Fujiyama,
Rodrigo (travelling) noticed a much calmer
Hind than the one he saw in city streets
(As New York's), whose few victories, many defeats,
Confuse Rodrigo as he earnestly tries
To find the Hind that hides whenever it spies
Rodrigo, who of course has never found
The Hind or captured it the world around.

Old Doctor Miller and His Medicine Show

He was a sketch! He struck me for a job
And maybe a loan—I sensed that coming, too—

"I been up and down the East coast and the West, too,
Thought I'd make a run by here." No job
Could then be forthcoming and I knew
What it would mean to him. His bravery
And brass might melt, but it did not, luckily;
I waited silently till he was through.

That silence made an awful lot of noise,
He did not hear it though because he spoke,
He did not hear it probably, for it broke.
Then he must have heard. "Well, I'll tell the boys
There's nothing doing. Sorry," he went on,
"We'll be fifty miles from here by dawn."

Her No Meant Yes

She shook her head, no, no, her forehead shook,
Her curls shook, even her small ears tremulously
Uttered dicta of negativity
And with her sideward eyes she gave a look
Of never, never, never utterly—

"There are commandments written in the book
That say, 'Thou shalt not take by hook or crook
What appertains to neither you nor me!' "

Though with her lips she uttered, "No, no, no,
It cannot be—it must be never so.
It is not mine to give nor yours to take.
Speak no word lest the teeming silence break
And the house of cards be scattered many a mile—"

All of it meant yes, yes, and all the while!

I'm Glad to Meet You

I'm glad to meet you, sir, my name is *me*.
I understand that your name, sir, is *you*?

Well, I do nothing. Tell me what you do?
(Nothing, I say, that is, I live and be,
Hence am human—are you human, too?)

Where do you live? Here, certainly, I see.
I live anywhere. And where are you bound to?
There? I am going to infinity.

Who are your people? He? And she? And they?
Everyone is my family. And why?

Well, you have yours for your posterity,
I have no one, more or less the pity.

Will we ever meet? One time, you say?
I say never, with equanimity

The Marsh

The marsh was purposeless, it lay inert,
Semi-narcosed its tideless water lay.
Only bubbles broke the muddy dirt,
With heat the checkerboard and sun to play,
Pushing its gambits in the face of day
Insects, animals, but no humans there.

The evening heard an orchestra of strange tunes
Sweep across the sea-pools toward the dunes
And as the night came on, the bass and treble parts
Winnowed together like two beating hearts.

Frog and cricket flung their violent darts
Of sound into the stricken autumn air,
While no mortal near enough to hear
Applauded the artists there for what they were.

Proverbial Swan

Lyric swan, upon this poplared lake
Whose lonely cubicle winds rarely shake,

In your noiseless cruise what shores have you
Let your webbed propellers bring you to
That tread the water soft and dark and green,
Mirroring back your snow and all the sheen
Icy-waxen, marble seen-unseen
Of your plumage;
          —water green and dark,
Cool in the sultry and midsummer park.

Lyric swan, to what shores are you come?

Margins of whose phantasy or dream
Stop your magical barge afloat upon
Noon's waters, that set out at early dawn
For what destination, cargoed one?

Fairy Tale

I heard a sound and hid behind a tree;
Would I be seen? Would any animal find
My scent? Would any fierce beast chance to hear
Me as he passed by with pricked open ear?

This was flashed on my bedevilled mind
In consternation and immediacy
To hide, protect me, as the four came near.
Who came near? I was hastening to tell:

Two maidens and two leopards sauntering
Passed twenty feet beyond me through the dell;
They were apparently daughters of the king
Of that region—both girls chattering
Like birds, the leopards, very dignified,
Treading most sedately at their side.

The Sky Sifts Dead Snow on a Dying World

Outside, but in the houses winter is
A dreaded name, a hungry wolf at a door
That never will be opened as long as fire
Stands between indwellers and the ice.

Snow is swept and blown and snow is whirled
Across the winter sky and across the winter
Earth, like petals from blossoms in paradise
In celestial meadows, and the kiss

Of cold lies still imponderable, still delaying,
On buried seeds that would go but must be staying,
Waiting a warmer touch than winter's hand
That holds fast-gripped the ice-locked frozen land,

Though indoors fire-flame leaps head-high and draws
On walls the shadow scenes of his lost cause.

How Do You Manage to Do It?

Time, what do you do when you are not
Ageing men and women, making them wise,
Tearing the veils away from human eyes,
Putting people to bed and permanently
Undoing everything, making cold out of hot
Pease porridge, drumming, drumming insistently
On the membranes stretched over centuries
(Like barrel-heads) and grinding persistently
With ocean as tool against geographies?

Time, you find white paper that is clean
And new, and you stain it yellow. I have seen
You do the same with lawns, with marble that was new,
With ivory, with skin; I have seen you do
It with immutable mutabilities.

"La Lune ne garde Aucune Rancune"

The moon arose as if she might assume
Dominion of the minions of the night:

The drowsy bat that wheeled in silent flight
And leaped and dropped—the moon would well illume
Its velvet back and have light left to spare,
To scatter silver largesse on the air,
To lift the tidal water anywhere,
Relieve the dark earth from its nuptial plight
(Deserted by the sun that shone with might
Through loud corridors of the noisy day).

Also she rose as if she were going away,
Taking her silver with her, going to stay,
Instead of as if she might deign to assume
Dominion over the minions of the night.

Eyes in Libraries

I observe peculiarities
In the movements of the human eyes
Over desks of public libraries.

Eyes there rove a bit more than is wise,
Often show inquisitiveness or surprise,
Notice gloves and shoes and socks and ties
And even query *whose* and *whats* and *whys*.

You can notice peculiarities
In the motions of the people's eyes
In and near to public libraries.

Men and women go there to sit and read
But they squirm and rove, survey each other
Not as sister, quite, and not as brother,
But more with nervous desire or anxious dread.

Some Moments Never Are Historical

In this slender segment of the world
Where the sky is more overcast than bright,
Leaves no sooner than they fall are whirled
Down into mould to live with the miner, Night,
Who digs into men's minds—but here I say
Occurrences, not too memorable to behold,
Take their place in the full glaring light
Above the surface of the teeming mould:

a) two ants attempt (unsuccessfully)
To carry off a crumb (too large) of bread;

b) seven geese fly by harmoniously
Forming a V (but roughly) overhead;

and c) a chained bull in the pasture near
Troubles the turf and stamps a large spot bare.

Lady, Sleeping

Your coverlet is white (no miracle there);
Your blanket is soft (no miracle in that);
The plateau of mattress is covered by a sheet,
Over which rise the mountains of your hair,
Valleys and crevasses dangerous
To all but the most intrepid one of us . . .

Your room is still (ordinarily it is);
Your window is open and silent; the street is
An empty square at midnight after the carnival
Meeting you always is and always was .   .

Yet your hands are folded flowers in the night that keep
A nameless perfume indeterminably caught
In chalices of the tenderness you brought
From the indescribable loneliness of sleep.

Out of Your Sky You Shot Your Bolt at Me

With the swiftness of the wind, with the arrogance of
    the stars,
Your vision crossed mine and I saw the bars
Of the endless prison out of which you lean.

Heaven, that night, and all the vault, was clean
Of immanences but one; still Lucifer
Shone where he was waiting there for her
And we could see him shining. And still you stood
Till I could hear the footbeats of your blood
Parading down your thronging arteries.

"This is the mystery of all mysteries,"
Something in me told something else in me,
And now is the time and the place. I cannot talk—
The silence is too hard for me to break;
I stood there stark and waited patiently.

Blind People Drink Water the Same as You

Their windows are blank phantoms that admit
The world's gross body—not the soul of it.

Wind and noise crowd in tumultuously
But everything outside for eye to see
Framed by this window—it remains outside.

Your majesties, I pray, do not deride—
Nor do be horror-stricken—those who stand
Serving and also wait; each in his hand
Holds a key to a door you may not enter
That leads to a room, where standing in its center
There is a table. On the table is
Mysterious water of all the mysteries,
In a glassy silver pitcher that imparts
Strength to souls and courage to sad hearts.

Do Your Christmas Shopping Early

I saw: the seriousness with which John Green,
The son of man and forty other things,
Looked in windows where were scattered rings,
Cigarette-holders, poker-chips, and dice,
Victor discs, and pocket radiophones,
Cards and flasks and scissors, every price,
And every class and kind; how Mrs. Green
Thought of how her dollars all had wings

As she watched, too; and how the little Greens
Looked at sleds and wagons painted blue,
Electric trains and steamships, toy telephones
And lights and tinsel, too bright to be true—
Until the crowds around them all had gone
And they, aware of it, stirred and moved on.

The Sky a Palimpsest

Record of the grey morning: the sky broke
The moment dawn's shaft entered; broke in two
And changed from deepest blue to lighter blue—

The color of a broken sky, irreparable
This one was; only a new sky could replace
The morning's figure and the morning's face.

Then the next step: what had been silent then
In symphonies of noise subdued began
To warble, twitter, to uncoil and run.

What had been still took motion for its part,
Slow-ticking heart became quick-beating heart,
The fires of night turned ashes, fell apart,

Then out of all this came on and on
Nothing but morning after merely dawn.

The West Façade of the Parthenon Tells It All

The birth of morning and the death of night
Are moments when I realize my plight;

My horses rise red-nostrilled from the sea
But only serve to mock and mortify me.

Mars is archaic, and the rest of them
Are near to his oblivion with him.

Venus is always ready to endow
Me with more than I can reckon now.

And Jove with splitting forehead only hands
Me out a measure to survey my lands.

Thus evening creates for me more than I spend
And twilight brings the play to a simple end;

Into the waves my horses plunge in fright
At death of daytime and the birth of night.

Imago

Image of my continual consternation
I cannot paint you in oils, oils are too thin;
I cannot carve you in marble, marble is too thick;
I cannot build you in a building; or with words
Say and keep you permanently, words are too quick.

Yes, there are portraits, but there is none like you.
There are descriptions of heaven-flying birds
In ancient manuscripts; there is the Taj Mahal
And carven statues as memorial

To beauty like your beauty: but with you
I find them all more feeble than my cry
Against the powerfully rebellious sky
That serves as your tent merely or as the place
Towards which at times you wearily turn your face.

O Glimmering World

O glimmering world, so dangerous, so bright,
With Time the sands that rim your seas are white;
And whiter on them bleach the gleaming bones
Of those you gnawed and polished, earlier ones

Than these that, garbed in muscle and in flesh,
Walk your streets today beside the sea
Besieging you with frantic cry and wish
For emptiness and for satiety;

And earlier too than those that are not born—
Unthinkable thought and unpronounceable name
Of unmined honor and of unreaped fame,
Of fruit unbudded, or unsprouted corn—

O glittering world, so dangerous and bright,
With Time the sands that rim your seas are white!

HEARING

The Papers

They tell me that a child is being beaten
And that a house is falling in decay,
That somewhere opium is being eaten
And that a ship is leaking in the bay
And that the city's sewers are too small
To carry the night-earth, and that the cost
Of building them again is money lost,
And that a book about Morgan le Fay
Is being written in a garret room
And that the enemy has scaled the wall
And that millenniums will surely come
And that an aged woman in despair
Has fallen headlong down her lodging stair
And that her yellow dog has run away!

Little Tommy Tucker Crooned for His Supper

He was not slow. It did not take him long;
First the tune, then the words that went with the song
He learned and began to sing them then and there:
"Too-ra loo-ra loo-ra loo-ra laire—"

And the more they listened the more they were en-
    chanted;
"Here is exactly what we all have wanted
So long now that we forget the day
We first decided we wanted it this way:

"You shall be commissioned, subsidized,
Musicians of your kidney should be prized!"

They made his name a byword in the town
Where he wandered slowly up and down,
Singing re-mi-fa-sol-la-ti-do
Everywhere that people let him go.

Andrew MacClintock

He told me he spent thirty-seven years
Alone in the cabin. During that time his ears
Never received the vestige of a word
From Caucasian lips. He told me he never heard
One English word from those he lived among,
That his eyes never fell on one who spoke his tongue;
That the tribesmen came, conversed with savage signs,
And brought him what they had tunnelled out of the
 mines.

"What was it like," I asked him finally,
"Never to hear a voice, never to see
A face that uttered your language, never to know
The sound of familiar words like *come* and *go*
And *yes* and *no* and *here* and *have* and *had?*"
"Oh, I couldn't complain," he answered, "it wasn't
 bad."

Liam's Post-encephalitic Parkinsonian Syndrome

On nights when the wind would blow in from the sea,
Heavy with deep-salt water and half-fog,
Liam turned off the radio, patted his dog,
Or fondled the master model of a sloop
He owned before his shoulders knew the droop
Now they were fixed to with rigidity.

He was always ready to listen, ready to be told
The story of Deirdre. Or, he sat in his house
In the woods and merely watched his friends carouse
With the music, liquor, and women that once were his.

Liam was not old, yet he was old,
He had a future, yet he had a history,
He was attended by all yet he sat alone,
Cold in a furnace-heated mansion of stone.

Sermon on the Mount: This Time from Station WZQX

With a rich, generous voice the preacher replied
(His voice was a roof, it rained in the world outside),

Speaking words to salve the world's wounded ego
From the sermon on the mountain long ago.

Thus contrived to pass the Sunday afternoon
By grace of rain outside and hearing the tune

Of water on eaves, in gutters, while inside
To every question of the world a voice replied

Over the wireless in this complicated age:
The voice declaring again against the wage

Of death for sin, a voice rich, generous
As a thick-roofed house when weather is tempestuous

Outside in the world—such a different circumstance
From when it was uttered on the mount by chance.

Neo-Classicist

He used Greek words because Greek words conspired
To rest the words that usage had made tired;
Words that were carefully nailed and carefully wired,
Built into his text as if inspired.

The saint, the story of the saint, the death of the saint—
Greek words rendered every detail quaint,
Greek words did for it as would have paint
Cautiously applied to colors faint

And dull by the passage of time; and men forgot
Whether they had heard the tale or not
And what they had thought about it, had they thought
About it ever, and where it was fought,
The battle, over its origin, and whether one ought
To include it among other classics that were bought.

Mosaic Made of Dinner Conversation

—Benjamin Bartlett will be there for dinner—
—Mrs. Papyrus diets to get thinner—
—Adam Weld bought her a motor-car—
—That young girl with blonde hair will go far—
—It is the quietest village that I know—
—The *Bremen* goes faster than *Berengaria*—
—The path was covered by a foot of snow—
—They claim that morphine made her hair turn grey—
—Only his glove was found in the locked room—
—Did you see Esmeralda when she was here—
—We were living there this time last year—
—Human bones were ploughed up out of the loam—
—No, I have not seen her. Is she gone?—
—That must be her lover sitting alone—

Coming of Herzl

You came to a community destroyed
By serpents and leopards, and you came
On sewers there that were stink-holes of shame;
The only weapon you carried was your name.

You being what you were—it was not safe
At times for you to walk alone down streets
After pay-day, or alone on Saturday nights;
But your fists were a protection, and your laugh.

Then you took the flower of your voice
And held it out for them to see, to smell,
Which they did, and were well entranced; then it befell
They listened to your voice, and as they did
Evil after evil arose and hid
(Leaving the place) their faces, as they were bid.

Will They Say—?

He is gone and they talk about him now that he
Is gone; when I am gone will they talk about me
In that way? What, then, will they have to say?

Will they say: He was tall; I never knew him at all.
Will they say: I knew him; he was not very tall;
He was of medium height. Will they mention me at all?

Or will anyone have measurements; will one say:
He was six feet tall on his twenty-first birthday,
He had brown hair, or, his hair was rather red
And was unruly over his ruly head,

Or will it be uncertainties they will say
About his hair; who will remember the way
It was, who will remember what he made
Of nothing in the sun and in the shade?

"S.S. *Titanic*"

Ears were listening, while the florid notes
Of brass trombones fell on the spotless deck,
With minds nearer to anything than a wreck,
Planning what they'd do when the ship would dock—
When suddenly it struck the berg. The shock
Collapsed the steamer chairs that were under some
And spilled the wine out of glasses they sipped from
And dashed their thoughts to preservers and life-boats:

The water pours in the gap made in the sides
Of the giant vessel—bells ring—signal lights flash on
In seven minutes the first boat-load is gone—
The second life-boat with the third collides—
Deeper she settles—prow dips under at last—
Stern rears and plunges—the episode is past!

Operator, I Want to Speak to William Trimbletoe

Hello, this is Thomas à Tattamus,
Hello, hello, are you there, hello!
William, this is Thomas à Tattamus,
This is Thomas à Tattamus speaking, hello,
Over the wires of literature that run
From your time and place in libraries to our own,
Over the skeins of person, place, and thing
That Fortunatus is busily unrolling;

I have a question, William, to ask you,
I have heard, and tell me, is it true
That Love is merciless, cruel, and unkind,
And Beauty painful?
                    Yes, you say *Love is blind*
And Beauty is a fiery dolour—I believe
What you say; I am sure the dead would not deceive.

Silent Night

Could a room be so still and yet contain
The living breathing body of a man?
It was and it did and Jack slept silently;

Peacefully, as the ship of the world careened
On through the dark of night to the gulf of dawn:
The sky stood silently over the silent earth
And the land stood silent by the silent sea,
Beside the silent sea stood the silent city
And in the city lay the silent streets;
Lining the streets the silent houses stood
And in this house Jack's body and Jack's blood
Breathed, pulsated as the universe slept,
As became a man, silent in a silent bed,
Alive and dreaming, sleeping and not dead.

This Was Trolje, Bleeding Her Heart Out

Through the noiseless house delirium
Spread like invisible fumes of a lethal gas;
The walls were arches of a proscenium,
Or a stage curtain, and let the weapon pass.

Delirium came into the still house;
Then invisible horns of silver and of brass
Sounded. A mortal would only have heard the mouse
In the attic, perhaps, but the invisible gas,

Delirium, continued to invade
The house; its occupants became afraid
Of the noisy woman's cries in the upper room,
Who tossed upon her low delirious bed
Whose four pilasters supported impending doom
Over the mattress into which she had bled.

O Time-Greened Copper Trumpets in the Hands of Grey Stone Statues on Rotting Church Cornices

Trumpets, that issue no sound, blow out upon
Cities populous with consternation,
Where men now exist and seekers seek
Reasons or a rhyme from out the wreck—
To find there only those disunified
Because of maladjustments somewhere in
Reciprocal relations lying between
People's hearts and other persons' greed,
Class hating class, distrusting, jealousy,
Chaos' birth, the death of destiny.

Ecclesiastic trumpets, you have failed
Above the cities; evil is not flailed
To yield some grains of wisdom, even pain
Has not yet taught you not to fail again.

The Rain-Crow is in the Forest

In the clump of poplars by the edge of the
Field, rain-crow, in late summer, early fall,
Is it there you rehearsed so long your call
That, now in perfect time and tone and all,
You emit it intermittently?

The fields are dry with August; on the leaves
Powdered summer sticks like blood on greaves
Dried; there has been no water for eight weeks—

However, your cry predicts a cloud that breaks
Later, that will break soon to let spill on
All of us a rain that lasts till dawn

And washes the dust from leaves and, in the road,
Turns what lately spun to mud that cakes
Upon wheels heavy with the harvest load.

That Voice

That voice is an old voice that has sung
Down centuries wherever bells are swung,
Or hymns in praise of deities are sung,
Or prayers issue from the facile tongue
Of priest or of unpriestly worshippers,

Who bring huge sacks containing all their fears
To set them down beside cathedral doors
And pick them up, when each one reappears
Outside the door, to take them back again
To their accustomed residence of pain

That sheltered each and roofed each from the rain
That also fell down the long centuries
Where voices echoed that were less than these
Today that lip absurd amenities,

Blurt Out Your Dreams

Here are the mind's truest geographies:
These words, the nets between them, and what else
Sounds like cymbals and resounds like bells
By no track, by no path that anyone sees.

The spider in his web is less obtuse
Than the deep intricacies between the thoughts
Of any man; less definite, less loose,
The mesh of Circe with its many knots.

Yet by these dreams, these free associations,
You weave a story that the consternations
Of many years have written with the quills
Of many hyacinths and daffodils
Beside the streams from many a garden pond
And open meadows that lie out beyond.

Then One of Those Terrible Silences Occurred

The guilty silence persisted and no one
Spoke and nothing happened. Noise was undone.
Unformed noise, also absent, was not heard.
There was no noise of hearts beating under coats,
No noise of sobs a-gathering in throats.
The silence hummed and roared, the silence purred.

What had caused the silence? When would it end?
Was no one clever enough to be a friend
To noise and deny the silence and bring noise back
And derail silence from the central track?

Then one of those terrible silences occurred,
One of those silences when no one spoke,
No one breathed, nothing whatever broke
The ominous absence of the uttered word.

Twitter of Swallows

Even horses cocked an eye upward, passers-by
Stared and the street-car conductor stopped and stared.
A child said: "The swallows act as if they were scared;
Maybe it means someone is going to die."

The swallows indeed seemed much excited about
Something, something, something—what could it be?
Here was an ordinary park, an ordinary tree,
The day had been an ordinary day,
And twilight fell quite unexcitedly.

But here were the swallows twittering, milling about,
Screaming as if a vital wrong were done
To each and all of them, as if the sun
Were stolen, nevermore to grace their sky,
Or as if the sun had gone away to die!

The Old Man Is Always There

No voice, no audience now, but the old man
Is still there in his house and very much
At home in spite of us and other such
Who see as little of him as we can.

Once, when we were young, when we had need
Of what he offered, of his meat and bread,
We were very glad to go and live
Where he lives and where he has to live.

But now our diet varies, there are many
Things we can procure with our penny
And we rarely see him—once a year
Or so we go and sit and listen and hear
Him say the same old things we used to hear
When he seemed so important to us there.

You Cannot Tell Young People Anything

When you are young you cannot ever be told.
You cannot tell what story will be yours.
The lighthouse keeper's lass that bent the oars;
You may be her in later seas that surge
Over your house and family. I urge
You well to remember that the boy who held
The leak in the dyke is not as dead today
As Sappho's or Euripides' cold clay;

Or the lad who tried to fly too near the sun,
Or Pandora's box, the midge-infected one,
Or the race that gained its strength from touching earth,
Or the maiden Zeus' headache gave to birth,
Or the Spartan boy, the fox beneath his belt—
These are all near enough now to be felt.

Continuous Exchange Between Men and Words

The exchange between men and between words
Of meaning, meaning, meaning, continues:
Men give it to words by using them,
Words give it back to men after they are dead.

Emotions may enter, listed, from love to dread;
They fly, they flutter, like so many birds—
But they are only words; noon-heats, dawn-dews,
Cannot dry and cannot moisten them

For they are words and words with meaning packed
By men whose souls are variously racked,
By men whose heads are variously thwacked
And yet from whom words, words with meaning, come
That men give words by merely using them
And that words give back to men when they are dead.

Lost

My song fell out of the miserly hands of Time
(Who has more music than he well can keep)
And was complete with letter, meter, rhyme,
And music definite and meaning deep;

It fell near where I stood, near to the place
My home had always been, but no one heard
It any more than one might hear a bird
Sing, if one were fasting in disgrace.

Then my prayer slipped from the ungenerous arms of
Time,
It bounded on the pavement, rolled away;
It was not a printed prayer-slip that would stay
Upon a tree in an oriental land,
Pinned to a withering tree by a faithful hand
And addressed to a god no longer in his prime.

Why Monuments?

I never heard of him; it is hard to see why
People should point a monument to the sky
Just to remember that one fellow by—
I know plenty who have done as much,

Or more. I know. Oh, you say he was the first,
Well? So what? It probably was the worst
Time it was ever performed. Everybody now
Does it and does it better anyhow.

What is the use, I ask you to tell me,
Of placing stones upon stones, and marked with bronze,
In memory of a man like you or me,
Or of building a building somewhere or planting a tree?

I might have seen some sense in it one time, once
I might have, but now it seems like foolishness.

Nightmare

Have you forgotten what the storm declared
In too loud a voice for your unstopped ears,
When eyes of lightning scrutinized your fears
And spoke with thunder as the only word?

Have you forgotten the all-overlooking face
That peered out of the sky upon your house,
Within which we were making frail carouse
Thinking ourselves securely set in place?

Then came the cyclone—it was the faces' breath—
Bringing to us oblivion, bringing death,
Blowing upon us, lifting us, carrying us
Into the north night, over the dark tremendous
Zones of Capricorn and over Cancer,
Gone—do you not hear me enough to answer?

Enfant Terrible: Heard at Vesper Hour

Creating beauty out of nothing but
The husks remaining after hogs are slopped—
Jesse, who devoured the bread you sopped
In whatever it was? O bare-brained beauty!

It took a woman finally to show duty
To your prodigal hands. Do not belie
The truth that I have come to know you by
And do not pause and gasp—"I don't know what

You mean by that!" I mean now what you mean,
If you mean anything I believe you do.

How do we get those ideas? How do they come
To anyone? Bees in rock amber? I'm not sure,
No one can say; let's disassociate
The factors that made us both be born too late.

I Heard the Rats Gnaw Through the Wall of Night

The rats begin to gnaw at nine o'clock;
By ten o'clock they are well at their task.
Eleven comes and then the hours ask
Will they never be finished? Then at midnight
The gnawing stops to be resumed at one.
At two o'clock the gnawing still goes on,
And at three the work is very much nearer done,
Though at four the night's myrmidons are not gone
For they gnaw till five to greet the entering sun.

They gnawed until they gnawed through the wall of
        night;
It cracked and fell and let the morning light
Enter and the terrific din of dawn
Was only the tumbling wall the rats gnawed on.
They left the scene when morning became bright.

SMELLING

That Faint Odor

Let's go to swim at midnight in the lake,
Naked, after the moon has risen up
Enough to show us half its yellow cup,

And reflections on the water quiver
In the silent pool by the rowan tree,
Overhanging, giving secrecy
To the mossy shore on the shallow side
Where small moon flowers now are opening wide,
In the pallid light of the waning moon
That dawn will despoil, overcome, pretty soon . . .

Now do you smell that faint odor like a spice?
I can tell you its source; the rattlesnake!
Some are nearby drinking, I've seen them twice
Before, once here and one time down the river.

The Water Smelt So Cold

The rain continued; it rose even higher,
Too high for swimming safely, though some went
Daringly as if to circumvent
The river-god's neglect-conditioned ire.

March was a cold month; with sharp fingers of rain
The sky grabbed, grappled, plunged at, struck the soil,
In a way that made mud puddles boil;
Clay hills furrowed and ravined under the strain.
Some boys went swimming then in Muddy River,
Dangerous sport—it made their muscles quiver,
The water smelt so cold; it could have been
Iced, or it could have been a bath of fire,
But nerves could not have told what the water was,
Under the pine trees full of cawing crows.

Grandfather's Morning is a Simple One

At eight he wakes or is waked by servant John,
Who hands him clothes and helps to put them on.

Then he breakfasts at nine, but not finicky
Is breakfast: eggs and bacon, coffee—why
Does Grandfather love food so? But he does!

At ten to his barber—O that paradise
Of scents and soap and clean, soft, heated towels.
And then the mysteries of Grandpa's bowels.

The sluggish day is only half begun
Without perusal of *The Morning Sun,*
Which done, these functions still remain: to walk,
To doze, to be critical, to watch the time, to talk . . .

Time has castrated Grandpa; his endocrines
Are of no more use than his *vas deferens.*

Smell of Cider

A hundred years ago a man named Jones
Lived here and made cider, people say,
Until the go-west fever stung his bones
And urged him up and took him out away
Beyond the Rockies and the desert dust,
Where people never die but dry or rust
And blow away, and settled him along
The deep Pacific where he heard its song.

Now here beside a spring in Tennessee
Remain his cider-press, his cotton-gin,
A few burnt bricks, a few stones from his home.

Fellow, where would you stay, forever be?
Mister, what barrier could hem you in?
Partner, who could unlearn your feet to roam?

There Was Another Planet

The Voice said, "Move on your accustomed path!"
The planet did not move. The Voice's wrath
Roared again, "Begone; commence; begin!"
It did not stir the stillness it was in.

"Will you not move along the course your brothers
Follow?—Will you not be like all the others?"

"Then I will crush you with my heavy fist
Until your particles are small as mist!"

The fist descended and the planet fell
Into a thousand pieces, some as small
As weightless motes, and some as meteors
To streak the dawn and dusky night with fires
That flash and glide and fade across the sky
As do rebellious thoughts in memory.

Aroma of Words

Now here are empty words for empty tongues
In empty mouths and empty heads to utter,
Shibboleths for overfilled hearts (and lungs)
And too-full throats and lips to shout and mutter.
All are here for old, young, rich, and poor,
Tall, wide, male and female, shallow and deep,
A treasury of words where Time will keep
Riches you cherish, prizes you desire
Until your eyes turn other ways than this,
Until your ears listen for different sounds,
Until your nostrils know new scents to miss,
Until your fingers reach for different bounds,
Until your lips learn other loves to kiss,
Until your feet lead you to other grounds.

TASTING

Lines in Hunger

Green earth, adjudicated forevermore
Only to be the threshold or the door
Through which we pass, and nourisher of grass,
And not be the holy, magic ball
We thought contained, we thought would give us, all
We wished for were it emptied to the core;

Green earth, why have you answered with a flame
The cry we thought to be your hidden name,
And burned our faces, scorched our tongues and ears,
Leaving us scarred and smarting, full of fears
To carry with us through the days we pass?

—Green earth, who gives to cattle and to crops
Pabulum, but only indirectly drops
Largesse upon us in our hungry years.

Food of the Gods We Want and Will Wait For

Inordinate conception of their greed
Gave ample reason for their hearts to feed
On nothing in the corners where they stood
And clamored petulantly for better food.

"Then what food would ye have, O deities,
Whose hearts are so great and your minds no less?
How did you live before you entered here
Where sea-snow and sea-sleet disturb your hair?"

"We fed by dew and manna, from the trees
Our houses were before inconstancies
Of steel and masonry erected all
The auditoria and banquet hall
Where we sit now envisioning new food
That will restore our sinews and our blood!"

Hurry Up, Drink and Food for King Cheops!

Hurry, because King Cheops has great thirst;
Hurry, fill his cup the very first,
It has been ages since a drink has flowed
Over his lips that one far day bestowed
Such high office on so many men—

It may be long many a day again
Before another follows this one down
The throat that has so parched and shrivelled grown—
Vintners, squeeze the juice as fast as you can;

Pluck the grapes and bring them, serving-man,
Because the king is waiting and he waits
Not as gracefully as brazen gates
Wait an enemy or a conqueror . . .
Hurry, before you rouse King Cheops' anger.

Morning, and American Breakfast to Top It Off

When morning comes the gold-fish bowl is changed
And books put back that evening disarranged.

Dust that the afternoon had settled down
Back in the air by the dusting-cloth is thrown.

The blinds are opened that the twilight shut,
Each chair and cushion in its place is put.

Windows are lifted and new air flows in
And the old air goes outdoors to stay again.

And so the day begins with cereal, coffee,
Fruit and cream and bran and orange juice.

The papers tell what you and I deduce
Of murder, arson, pillage, rape, suttee.

And down the street invested warm and fair
Jauntily stalks the morning debonair.

Backyard

We never would keep the fish from Graveyard Pond;
We caught them there but always threw them back
Or let them dry to rot on the railway track
That ran through Emmit to the towns beyond.

We caught the fish, they always did bite well
There in the Graveyard Pond, but we were afraid
Because spring water near the graves would swell
And taint the fishes somehow from the dead.

Only the Negro children ate the fish.
They did—also one white boy from the town
(Who was birth-injured, a half-wit silly clown)—
Baked in clay in ashes from a wood fire.
They knew and told us much of their desire,
Yet ate forewarned and gratified their wish.

Fistful of Bread

So breakfast actually was break fast to him,
That watcher, for as dawn broke through the dim
Firmament he stood where he had stood,
For centuries presumably, though only
One night in reality, on the edge of the wood
Of Bravabar.
              He stood and watched with eyes
Wiser than the sleeping world is wise
For something he did not find, he did not see;

He saw only trees, despair, and only the lonely
Rocks, the desolate grass, abandoned weeds
Of summer, then he went back to his fire.
And, as the morning sun swam up and higher,
He baked him a pone of bread made from the seeds
Of corn, and ate it to cinch his fidelity.

The Starving Man

When the world is dark and the moon is only
A lantern behind a veil of mist, your lonely
Lighted window stands set into the night
Like a topaz on ebony for Cyclops' delight,

And it sings a song where only silence is heard
Like the pulse of the stars, or the shadow of a bird
Over a lake, over forest and meadows winging,

Or laborers chanting at their work and singing
After their valiant bread, their water sweet

As are the prints left in sand by your feet,

Or the taste to a starving man of meat in tins,
Cakes in boxes, ale in nipperkins—

As ever along the banks of Time's deep sea
The waves rise, the waves fall, incessantly!

Celebrate the Vine

I would celebrate the lowly vine;
I would celebrate the vine because
It can confute so many foolish laws.
It, the mother of vinegar, father of wine—
Those opposites of life's drink, as you recall—

Vinegar sopped the sponge after the fall
Of Jesus, after the wedding where he turned
Water, the simple stuff, into richest wine,
Wine the result and wine the ardent cause
Of subjective triumph and objective fall.

I would celebrate the fruit, the vine,
Here because of heaven and also because
Of hell, because of order and the laws
That moulded it out of chaos: Evoe! The Vine!

How Water Freezes

Its fiat must be ready, its fiat is
Freeze; it freezes; tiny spicules run
From the edges inward like a pin
Of glass; from these, darts sideward leap and meet,
Then frost declares the world is fallen his,
And thin water now is hard and cold and sweet.

In the beginning ice was much as now
(Tempora mutantur) and the face
Of earth, except for rivers and the snow
Rarely changed in permanence their place.

Have you not seen ice graven upon stones?
King Solomon placed ice among the precious ones,
Though he had never seen nor tasted it;
It subsided as heat wasted it.

These Days

It is hard to keep a tradition in these days;
A person must eat, the body must have a bed
To lie in at night, a roof must be over the head.
There is a way and there are ways and ways.

The stomach will shrivel if it is not filled at times.
When it shrivels other members shrivel too;
The only thing to prevent it one can do
Is not to think romance, not to feed on rhymes,

But go find bread, And where is bread to be found?
Not as manna lying on the ground!

Sell the family portraits, what good are they?
Sell the gold clock that stood in the drawing-room.
They are better to go than face a doom
That cannot be postponed another day.

Here Is a Book That You May Call Myself— I Do Not Know and Cannot Gain Your Say

For I am not what I was yesterday
Nor the day before, as Thursday's kitchen shelf
Differs from Wednesday's by a can or two,
A bottle or box that went into the stew.

The point I make is only that NOW marks
A certain point in one's life that barks
Fiercer than it bites—apologies
Are better made to friends than enemies,
Et cetera, so why should we go on

Holding an inquest on a date that's gone,
For I could turn, I could be venomous
And say: The chief regrets that make me grim
Are not these poems and their vanities
But the thought of other people reading them.

Sans Souci

Slowly the dragon came and slowly ate
The world he stood on out from under him.

In one gulp the Spanish peninsula
Disappeared. The dragon crunched with vim.

Europe disappeared at the next bite,
Then Asia followed and then Africa
Down his throat. To wash the continents down
Atlantic and Pacific both were thrown
Into the red gulf of the monster's mouth;

North America followed them, then South
America, Australia, and Greenland,

The South Pole, next, the North, its ice and sand,
Then in one last mouthful went the rest of the world,
And he hung footloose where the globe had whirled.

FEELING

Summer Evening

He fell apart in three primary pieces
And sat there in the silence on the grass,
Listening to the ripple of moments pass
Or to occasional crickets that with kreeses
Of shrill exuberance cut the odorous air,
And he watched the moon above the flower-hung wall
Whose trumpet-vines and vines of honeysuckle
And morning-glory vines framed the ships in the bay
Beyond the wall that twinkled.
                                            There he sat,
Body and mind and spirit suddenly
Split, each to its part, and listening
To crickets, smelling perfume, and watching lights
Along the shore three hours after sunset;
And none of the evening's duties done as yet.

I Wish to Go into a Cavern Where There Is a Limited Quantity of Air

I wish to stay within the cavern till
The air is thin and used and I am ill;

I wish the cavern portal sealed to be
Dangerously and fatal unto me;

I wish to fall along the cavern floor
Using the air until there is no more;

I wish to use in its totality
The oxygen available to me;

I wish to make no effort to escape
No matter how I suffocate or gape;

I wish to stay within there till I die
And never have it opened by and by;

Which is the neatest and the simplest death
I know, and by the ministry of breath.

Yet There Are Parts of You That I Do Trust

What dark Euclidian chambers your eyes are
That see from me here to the Evening Star!

I trust them yet in spite of what I see
They know withal, that they perceive in me;

I trust your fingers though your fingernails
Are darkly flagellant as whetted flails!

—I trust your fingers though I do not trust
Your wrinkled visage seamy, lined with dust
From roads you travelled where I will not go,
Whether they are drifting deep in sandy snow
Or whether with summer's powder or fall leaves
They are rimmed; and strongly I distrust again
Your mouth, that orifice of continual pain.

These tell me loudly of your character!

Convalescent from Otitis Media

His illness was uncounted hammer blows,
Her nursing was a gentle restraining hand
She gave him; he was slow to understand
But now, out of delirium, he knows

What grace the water was she brought him there,
What charity the combing of his hair
And love the pillows were she helped prepare
In the nights of long and arduous

Pain and sweating to the hopeless dawns
When lethal vapor stood about the lawns
And entered the cubicle where he reposed
With the shades of senses shut and closed,
Long since winter and the winter snow
Went the way that he had feared to go.

Go! Letter!

Letter, lovingly addressed, lovingly sealed,
Lovingly stamped and carried, lovingly put
Into a mail-box near a gutter where soot
Soils the snow to February slush annealed,

Letter be then forgotten, then concealed
In memory—trustingly dispatched and set
Against a situation and in debt
To chance considerably,
                           —letter revealed
To be the bearer of a message from
One whose heart is a municipal garden
With only pleasure seekers and no warden
To one whose heart is a state prison grim,

Go, letter!—Go like a rapid dart
To the chained heart from the sunlit heart!

Until a Voice Behind the Altar Spoke

All night before the altar in a dream
I stood aware that any moment might
Bring a cancellation of that night
And let a light from over the altar stream
Onto my armour vesting me in white.

I was the priest, the walls however were
Abusive as water falling in a pool,
They called insultingly: O shallow fool,
There is no light, no answer to the call
You utter but the candle's wavy smoke!

Until a voice behind the altar spoke
And cried: Stay calm, stay patient, nothing is
Synonymous with all these prophecies,
The walls of time contain my histories!

It Is Time to Go Home and Go to Bed

Call a cab; the street is dark tonight,
Morning is about to enter with its light,
And you should be at home and safe in bed
Before the east turns grey and later red
With dawn and the sky grows brighter overhead.

Better call a cab for it is still night,
Past midnight, and trust your body to
Its recess that spins over park and row
Homeward as your tired members go
To their domicile upon a street
Silent now and quite devoid of feet.

When you arrive, pay the cab-man, take your key,
Enter the house, climb upstairs silently,
Undress, turn out the light, and go to bed.

Daring Cousin, Killed in an Air-Crash

Your fatal flight, your monument of no war!
So this was what you were preparing for
In the hours of maternal dark,

In the mornings playing in the park,
As a school-boy sitting at your desk,
Later on the athletic field, the risk
Then of mountain climbing in the Alps,

Then lion-hunting later, lion whelps
As pets, your motor-boat, your hydroplane,
And now this last concussion of your brain
Leading to a cemetery in the rain . . .

The meaning is . . . the meaning is . . . it is . . .
I halt to tell you what the meaning is;
I am uncertain that I know what it is.

The Cold Night Air

The cold night air flowed in and nothing stirred
In the room. In his mind no unuttered word
Echoed and no memory of any song
Clanged as he lay tirefully and long
On the bed beneath the thin quilt's kiss.

The moon shone in the window, the moon and the
Cold night air he breathed delightedly;
The moon was full and full of the moon was he,
And tired, in the silence going to sleep,

After a day no shepherd and no sheep
Had ever known; never in Illyria
Had such days been, nor in Etruria,
As this day in nineteen hundred and thirty-two
With a great deal done and a great deal yet to do.

Salutation to a Father from a Son

The impresario of this moment is
Your attitude in my memory, in my mind;

I remember you kindly and unkind,
Bald or capped with a bright Turkish fez;

Captain of my regiment that were thoughts
Enlisted in a land and far away
From the ocean that was my memory—

There were castles walled and rimmed by moats
But you took all of them and you can keep
Their donjons locked within your rooms of sleep,
Until they sleepless die and their men are gone
Into avenues of carven stone
Wider than day is wide and longer than
Night is long to sick and lonely men.

Fire of the Rocks

And, when no words fall from mellifluous lips,
No words, no kisses, but silence and no greeting,
Rein in the horse of your heart that has been beating,
Stop the cart of your mind that carries what you know,
And proposition both with insignificant quips
Uttered carelessly, as if no knife
Slowly cut the strings that held your life
Suspended over Oblivion's Abyss.

And try to train your fortitude to grow
Big enough to cover what it must,
Or if that fails, then grind away the rust
Time has eroded from the white blade of your will
And see if it is good to fight with still,
Then fight forever with the emptiness!

Forever and Forever and Forever

The grind of waves against the sandy beach,
The sweep of clouds across a windy sky,
The glide of other stars that pass us by,
The rush of comets that recede, approach,
The drift of current down the winding river,
The course of sands across an unnamed waste,
The million feet that tread a million roads,
The million prods given by a million goads,

Will it never cease—will it rest ever,
Even at some mute deity's request?

Will the hand never be silenced? Folded?
Will the mobile features never be molded
Into a still image, a grave face
That stands and watches expressionless the mad race?

Not for the Waking Eye

Now when the fingers are confused in sleep,
Concerned with dreaming, no one can predict
More easily than one could contradict,
Their course, for fingers that are half asleep
Are apt never to hold or never keep
What they have grasped, or might grasp, when asleep.

The counters that they pass a-groan with goods,
The tables reeling under many foods,
The various vintages, the various bloods,
The endless images on the trestle-board
Set out for sales that sleep and dream afford;

Unfortunately, these can never be
Brought from the dream for the waking eye to see
Or use and enjoy in reality.

Reunion, That Has Not Yet Taken Place

You promised me that if you could return
You would—and so I felt my fingers burn
Feeling you near. The dawn had not begun
To wake the chamber for the early sun
So I divined that you could not be far
From where you used to be and always are.

Tonight I almost let you in my room,
Someone was there—it might not have been you,
But in the darkest corner and the gloom
I felt your presence strongly and I knew
That, ever if mortal might have been so blest,
You would have answered my long-prayed behest
To see you once more—when you went away.

It seems as though it happened yesterday.

Unfinished

Honor, honor, where is honor fled?
Honor, honor, where is honor? Dead?
Leaders are come but where is honor led?

Men are born, nations grow; war, poverty
Descend like seasons on humanity;

One man avails little against the sea,
The tidal-wave, the flood of iniquity
That seems to flow.
                    King Knut is in his grave;
His word, his council did not help to save
The least or greatest from dishonor's grave—
Knut's failure then is not what we must have.

Can Darwin or Lenin possibly (or possibly Freud?)
Let us know where honor is unalloyed?
We are a people not with honor cloyed.

Yet Not to Death or Even the Limit of Living

I am tired of seeing my face; I am fatigued
At shaving my face, considerably indisposed
At washing my face, my body, combing my hair,
And of having it cut about once every two weeks,
Of brushing my teeth and using dental floss,
Seeing the dentist and having cavities filled,
Seeing a doctor and therefor being billed,
Buying clothes and wearing them, wearing them out,
Sitting in all kinds of chairs, lying in beds,
Putting hats on and off my several heads
(For business, for sport, for practice, for poetry),
Of ingesting food and later disposing of it,
And of having clothing altered so it will fit,
In fact, I am tired of living, but unwilling to die.

Faun Face

The impudent face of a faun had set Estelle
Adrift upon a sea of mesmerizing
Herself, until her vessel came near capsizing
Herself and it upon reality,
The sharp rock that held up the angry sea;
Her hunger was for love—that sea would swell
And more and deeper pound her heart. Estelle
Was tossed and drifted more than turbulently
Upon the waters of her hopeless sea.

The face of a faun had done that to Estelle,
It seemed; the face of a faun or even less,
The thought of a face of a faun, could so distress
Her mind she could not sleep until she had
Been tossed and drifted, tossed and shipweckèd.

Deep into Sleep, Asleep

Deep into sleep as into a coal-mine,
A pit of salt, a sulphurous abyss,
Sank Proteus (you might know more of this
If more of your experiences were his) . . .

So Proteus descended into sleep,
Into its cul de sac he settled down
And found it a silent hall, a silly town,
Still and colorless or shrivelled brown,
A sort of dungeon and a kind of keep
He floated to . . .
                . . . He could not move his hands,
Open his eyes, cry out, or traverse lands
He knew no name for and no burning sands,
But only sleep in the still and marvellous place
Where he encountered dreaming face to face.

Carter McCarter

While I knew him Carter suffered a wound,
Received beside a stream from a bright sword;

The stream was a city that flowed gently on,
The sword was from a dweller, a keen word.

The word had come out of a sky that shone
Warm as summer on the morning ground,
But it struck Carter's heart sword-like, and cut
Initials of the speaker there, and ground
What was left of the heart beneath the heel
Of him who spoke. Carter was first to feel,
The one always who felt, the last to feel,
And never to forget the pain from that quick word . . .

I think of him by cities now when steel
Is being forged and moulded into a sword.

Literature: The God, Its Ritual

Something strange I do not comprehend
Is this: I start to write a certain verse
But by the time that I come to its end
Another has been written that is worse
Or possibly better than the one I meant,
And certainly not the same, and different.

I cannot understand it—I begin
A poem and then it changes as I write,
Never have I written the one I thought I might,
Never gone out the door that I came in,
Until I am perplexed by this perverse
Manner and behavior of my verse.

I've never written the poem that I intended;
The poem was always different when it ended.

Appointment; Meeting; Then the Warm, Bright Room

With that air with which a man looks for
A woman, Rudolf stood in the cold street
And waited while the clouds spat rain and sleet.

He was poised, wordless, hat-brim over eyes,
Collar of coat turned up and no surprise
At or interest in other passers-by.

Rudolf stood in the gloom just outside of
The halo from the arc-lamp on the muddy street,
Watching and waiting, occasionally stamping his feet.
It was not idyllic, but the night was for love.

There was a meeting planned, an appointment,
It was understood and agreed together,
Time would bring the woman, time had brought the
        weather:
She came, space ceased, and time stopped for that day.

The Children Watch the Evening Train Go By

The train sounds like it's excited or worried or some-
 thing,
The way it moans on the rails coming down through the
 gap,
The whistle blows like it might mean something dan-
 gerous
And it grinds on the ties. The engineer waves his cap
As he passes us, then the last car—the brakeman is
 waving
His flag at the children, at the eleven of us,
Children of the neighborhood, watching the train go by
And listening to its noise of anxiety;

Why should we vaguely feel, as all of us do,
Watching the train rushing down the isolated valley,
That something is ominous, something impending, too,
That a daemon or evil spirit is apt to sally
Forth on the air to astound us as we stand
Holding each other for comfort by the hand?

Sleep's Blossoms Bloom the Best in Utter Dark

Sleep's blossoms bloom in light but better in
Darkness, for their soil is the thin
Dust of dreaming, grain by grain, that falls
In our courtyards from the inner walls
Of the stiff houses time has built in us
By moments vanquished or victorious—

Whether or not they finally are adjudged
So to remain or always are begrudged
By unfortunates who quickly spy,
Through our windows in the twinkle of
A lip, an eyelid, or an active eye,
Enough of truth to hide a larger lie

Though sleep's blossoms grow, still bloom and twine
Their tendrils over your trellis, over mine.

Did You Retreat?

Did you retreat before the empty house,
The vacant one with doors and windows closed,
Did you once, the one where you were used
To know well every soul that dwelled within?

You went there—not a sign—no rustling mouse,
No animal, no light streamed from within,
And they were no longer there who had lived within;

The street was dark and near to six o'clock,
A pall of smoke, some mist hung in the street,
You walked up to the door with resounding feet
But you did not stay, for no one answered your knock

And you have not learned where they were: they were
      away,
The bell rang hollowly in the silent house,
You did not think it worth your time to stay.

Time's Torrent Trusted

The javelins that hurrying years have hurled
Against my tower and against my wall
Are all forgiven, all forgotten, all
Their wounds are healed, and every pennant furled,
With the temporary flags of truce I raised
Against a force too strong to be appraised
That Time brought in, that with the militant years
Assailed my surety and changed my fears.

Since now they are forgotten, are assuaged,
The tempests and the torrents all have raged
Beyond my state, and my condition is
Becalmed in wiser words than centuries;

Chronos speaks truthfully to me now and I hear
His comfortless voice with an attentive ear.

Now, You—

Now, if my love were swallows, now the sky
Would be agloom with them until I die,
And in their twitter nothing could be heard
Forever but your name, the only word
I ever found that can transmute the merd
Of everyday and everyday's trite life
Into the golden stuff of ventured strife
With nothing to lose but everything to deny.

And if my love were robins then no grain
Would ever lie again where it had lain,
So thick their flight would cover the dull earth
With their bright heads and eyes, searching you out,
To where you are embowered, grace and mirth
And loveliness, and where I wait without.

Long Sonnet: Walking with Miss Emma

There was a mournful certainty with which
She used to close her eyes, and when I saw
Her coming down the walk toward me I knew
That with that manner or another such
She would accost me, tell me of the day,
Inquire of my annexes and relate
The interminableness of her prescribed delay
And what was often called her tireless fate.

There dwelt a sad assurance in her face
She must have learned from Mona Lisa's smile,
And often when we'd gone perhaps a mile
With it she'd turn to me and say, "Good-bye—
I've walked far enough now, must be going back!"
And we would part. She did that with the knack
Of having put it off, perhaps that I
Might have found other ways to end it by.

Contract with Life, Consideration Being Death

Life I love; I am its devoted slave;
I would possess all that I do not have;
Though I would carry nothing to the grave
It all returns, all that I ever gave.

Sunrise, sunset, noonday, and midnight,
Each is my terror, each is my delight;
I would sweat with love and freeze with fright,
If I could record them for you aright.

Take my scepter, Time, my watch, my ring,
My hand, my eye, my ear, my anything
But leave me living, let me live to live
And you are welcome what I have to give
(Except the pulse, the never-sated thrill
Of hill to climb and will to climb the hill!)

Surgery of the Liver

You cannot undo Liver, you can take
A finger off, a leg; make and remake
The nose, the ear, the face; break and unbreak
A compensating heart, fake and refake
A joint disabled or a stomach-ache
But Liver (Hepar), Liver must go on
Importantly as fifth wheel in the machine
Playing its rôle for every body's sake:

I must be here in beady drops of bile
Liver says (its only way to talk);
Liver says *I will not run, I will walk*
In my predestined way and all the while
I plod for you, you may run many a mile,
But O your slowness if I ever balk!

KNOWING

How Could I Know?

I did not know this was the crucifix,
This piece of wood, these simple transverse sticks,
I thought they might be household furniture,
They might have been the fragments of a chair;

Nobody told me, I thought everyone
Might be or do the same, that anyone
Might be much more or less, or that someone
Else might have it happen to them, but that I
Should be the one—I had not thought that I
Should have been it, but that some other one . . .

I thought while one was being crucified
One flung one's arms or shouted or outcried,
I had not thought, I had not realized
That it was I was being crucified.

You Will Know the Truth for He Will Tell It

In his last word, if you can be there,
Its odor will so taint the chamber's air,
It will rise so heaven's men can smell it,
It will so stink, what he can tell you there,
It will malperfume and darken the air.

He has known and carried it all through
India's jungles and the deserts of
Africa, seas below and mountains above,
As he travelled; he has carried it
Through his life alone but he will tell it
As he dies if you are standing there;

It will not be pleasant, what you hear,
The story of his hopeless tragedy,
But then he will feel free and ready to die.

And So

And so someone declared, *and so* someone
Mentioned at the juncture of the sun
With Silence and some others muttered loud.
And so declared the voice behind the cloud.

And so they faltered at the postern gate.
And so the ones declaimed who were too late
To board the vessel, *and so* they affirmed
Who saw the mud-mark where the dragon squirmed
Ages ago, *and so* they added who
Knew the secret formula of dew.

And so they asked who minded all the sheep,
Who were the prisoners within the keep
Of Zeus upon that mountain where the wind
Cooled them off and blew onlookers blind.

There Are the Strangest Apertures

I know the strangest apertures are made
For those to enter who are not afraid:

Grave-mouth with grave-stone firm upon it laid,
Or feet of idols where one can, dismayed,
Stand beneath their tall and weighty mass
And know the future as it comes to pass;

Often within dark Egyptian tombs
In my fantasy I closed the rooms
Where the king was sleeping and have gone,
Past the gilded stairway of rare stone,
To the travelling rooms where victuals were
And sampled them that were to have gone far
Into that land of life beyond the life
Where simple day takes simple night to wife.

The Answer to That

The answer to it is that people *do* starve,
That people do die in wretchedness and pain.

They have little gardens where they work in the rain,
And occasionally someone finds enough time to carve
His initials on a tree trunk, and there were times
When one was known to put a bullet in his brain.

People do all these things and a great many more
Recorded things and still a great many more
Unrecorded things and still a great many more
Unbelievable things and still a great many more
Unknown things—that even you do not know.

There is not any end; I doubt if there was a beginning.
There has always been (always will be) righteous be-
     havior and sinning,
And the answer to it all is: some are well fed and some
     starve.

The Dangerous Is Easily Achieved

You have achieved the danger you deserve;
The pot of earth the years do not conserve
Is yours to spill, is yours to save or pour
Upon the garden or beside the door.

Deep into death was your consistency
Ordained, before the lintel and the moat
Were set beside your pool where lilies float,
And your domain fell into bankruptcy

Of hands and thought, before your slaves were set
To be the forfeit of a silly bet
Made between two drunk men, and the noise
Of your despair became the sound that cloys
The ear of Jupiter, the father of
The gods that rose and fell for lack of love.

One of the Brothers Travelled on the Continent
During the Civil War

While you were doing that, our ankles stood
Deeply in icy mud at Bloody Pond;
The water turned dark red with our best blood
And drowned the names of which we were most fond.

Cannon belched fire and hot lead broke our joys;
We toyed with death and death played back at us.
Though we lost more than half of all our boys,
The last day came to us victorious.

While you were in Paris: opera, chocolates, furs,
Women and music, wine and warmth and meat—

Straw was too fine to bind about our feet,
Horses, too rare to eat, a glance of hers
Would have been paradise as the winter cold
Insisted that we were dying—that we were old.

Foreclosure

Here in the last dark chamber of my brain,
I close these objects that have caused me pain,
And have hope never to open them again:

Shattered hearts with pieces strewed asunder;
Mouths incapable of uttering wonder;

Lightning and her noisy groom, the thunder;
Dawn returning, and the hour before the dawn;

The tomb where into all my love is gone;
The massive hand for whom I play the pawn;

The cradle in which I rocked my youngest hope;
My oldest despair, executor, the rope;

Faces that have ceased to record their surprise;
Lids and the lashes of fear-tenanted eyes;
The tongues of bells that told me when to rise.

Free

Hierarchies of torn clouds that still
Mirror the water, mirror the moving mill.
These have ruled me longer than I would,
But I did not escape them when I could
And now the day is far that I may flee
This yoke of visions—hill and wood and tree
Command me as they will and I obey
Tomorrow and today and yesterday.

And why should I rebel? My feet are shod
With that green present carpet of the sod
And I am fed on milk and honey dew
Which is more than the nourishment that you
Are fed on; I am free to come and go,
Covered by thunder, heralded by snow.

Convocation

Into this room these objects four I bring:
The eagle first who instructed me to sing
And taught me how. Then his holiness, the snake,
That taught the day to fade, the dawn to break,
Who in his wisdom conquered everyone
That rose to strike him. Then his grace, the sun.
And then the arrow that a god has shot,
Staying perhaps in the heart, a vulnerable spot.

This room recipient, these four symbols here
Will never be gotten together again this year:

The eagle, who has far away to fly;
The arrow, who has to help a warrior dic;
The snake, who has tomorrow to prepare;
The sun, who has to go and warm the air.

If Fate Will Let Me Be

Out of the infinite vanity of my skin,
Out of the interminable mockery of my bone,
Lead me, Ego, toward the modest ones,
Guide me, Ego, among humble ones.

My muscles are strong with vulnerable stupidity,
My teeth are keen with edges of deceit,
Hollow and shallow is my entirety,
Cowardly, ostentatious are my feet.

But I have a core—a tenuous golden thread
Hanging from the ceiling of my head
That makes me worth enough not to destroy—

Clasp it, claim it, divide it, girl and boy—
I saved it for you, for you to save and save me—
Simple, that is, if Fate will let me be!

Your Diagnosis, Lady, Is Pregnancy

The two lamps of her eyes burned brighter then
Than they had burned the day she had known, when
Her breasts might feed a mouth she hoped to make
A richer ruby than the throat of the drake
Or the crest of the woodpecker. She stood watching.

What of her first-born—would he be a boy?
What would she name him—could she stand the joy
And the pain that would precede it, as she was now?

These and the distance to the Morning Star,
A small bright point and a glittering thing,
Were what her mind revolved on, these, and how
She might still learn the easiest way to bear
The precipitate hounds of the future that fawned to
        meet her,
The snarling wolves of the past that leaped to greet her.

Listen

You would not have done as I have done,
You could not have run the race I have run,
Leaping—I can feel it now—and sprinting,
Running, dashing, speeding with the wind,
Perilously hurdling boulders, logs,
Sidestepping nettles, arrows, barking dogs,
Furiously fleeing, and, barefooted,
Dodging obstacles as firmly rooted

As any forest oak that you could find,
As any head-on blustery buffeting wind,
As any river current, any tide,

And so it is my feet have finished printing
The welcome dewy grass of the domain
That now I know as the kingdom of your pain.

History of the World

It is written down, recorded here,
Sealed, affixed, and witnessed, stamped and signed.
Every detail is there, things as they were,
The wave, the cloud, the air, the sea, the wind.

All is inscribed and nothing more survives
That has no record; all the billion lives
And how each threaded its small way about
This monstrous maze and finally got out.

But look you, look! The Book, itself, has broken!
Like Moses' tables—marble is too weak
To bear a tale so ominous and bleak!

What matter then? A trillion books like this
Would be too few to hold the mysteries
That are written in the language never spoken.

Fable

Does everyone have to die? *Yes, everyone.*
Isn't there some way I can arrange
Not to die—cannot I take some strange
Prescription that my physician might know of?

No, I think not, not for money or love;
Everyone has to die, yes, everyone.

Cannot my banker and his bank provide,
Like a trust fund, for me to live on inside
My warm bright house and not be put into
A casket in the clay, can they not do
That for me and charge a fixed per cent
Like interest or taxes or the rent?

No, Madame, I fear not, and if they could
There might be more harm in it than good.

Call, Ask, Find

Call to the weavers. Ask the weavers if
You may ply with them and do their work.
If the weavers say no, then to the fishers
And their tiny shops along the mart,
Or to the dungeon and the burly bailiff—
You might help him hold his prisoners.

Or the philosopher with his alchemy
Might use your arms to bring wood to his fire.
Go to him because philosophy
Often employs heads that are for hire.

And if you find no remedy, no surcease
For the energy bursting in your heart,
Go alone then into the woods of darkness
Where each practices his silent art.

Dusty Miller's Predicament

This is the reason that I cannot go.
You see, the River Now is running slow;
After the spring rain and its tributaries
The creeks stopped flowing swiftly, and the snow
Melted from the slopes of Porphyro
That feed them, and the Swedish mercenaries
Came and killed the cattle, ate the crops
Fighting for the king. The river stops.

I cannot go because my river stops,
I cannot come, I cannot go, I stay;
My fate is tied to the river's fate, today
I know it plainer than ever. It turns my mill
And grinds the corn for the village over the hill
And makes meal, bone and muscle out of the crops.

Edward Moseback is a Gardener

What a man is not does not prevent
Him from being what he is. A king
Once declared he wished he had been born
Into the household of a cabin, where
He might have leaped to seize a hoe at morn
Instead of a scepter and have had the care
Of kine and fowl and daily gardening
While the humble seasons came and went.

But what a man is does prevent him from
Being what he is not—because you are
What you are, you are a gardener
And not a monarch: fife and horn and drum
Never will be your heralds, though the hum
Of bees may fill the garden when you come.

To Be in Liquidation

To be in liquidation means to be
In the state of being liquidated, see?
It's like this, or it's something like this, you see:

The World, The Evening World, and *The Sunday World*
Withered like trees. Their topmost leaflets curled
As if a blight had scorched them. I don't know why—
Was it circulation? I don't know. Maybe it was. Maybe
It wasn't that. Maybe it was something else; how do I
    know?
Maybe it was the times or even more complicated
Economic causes, like some say Troy fell
Because it was something or other about wheat.

All I know is I used to take *The World*
And I used to like to read it every day.
I've missed that paper since it went away.

So What?

Men, gross creatures, burly, prominent,
Are subject to small laws and smaller fates:

Witness the ways that accidents crush their pates
And will until Time finds a better way
To utter dicta that it has to say:

Item: Mr. Smith, president of Copper, Inc.
His motor skids, is wrecked, he bleeds and dies
Out of the thin cracked bones that were his skull
Not built to stand unnatural violence,

Nor will those ever be pearls that were his eyes
(Crushed jelly-berries—ugh!). I beg you note
The truth of what I say above; I wrote:

Men die from tiny causes even when
They are the poorest or the best of men.

Vincent Sturgeon

I am a man who has sat up too late
The night before; today is the morning after.
I am too tired to enjoy smiles and laughter,
Too sleepy to be patient or to wait
For what I know tomorrow means to bring,
Too weary to be mean or to be great
(If I might) or to be anything
If I would. And I would not because
I have learned the futility of laws
And that the death of desire lies in getting
What it was the appetites were whetting
Themselves for an hour ago and are forgetting
Now as stupidness and vanity—
That is what my zest has come to be.

Old King Betrayed

As he lay fevering, sleepless in the dark,
Thinking of time and all that it had brought,
Outside the palace dogs began to bark
And a tremendous brouhaha was wrought.

Then the dogs were silenced, something entered,
The court grew still. Was every animal cowed
Including the sentries that he kept on guard?
Thinking furiously the king's head bowed.

Now the defiant dogs resumed their din;
Something was crossing, had crossed, the courtyard.
The sentries? Drugged or bribed or sleeping hard?
His somewhat clearing mind began to work:

This is my terminal illness. That is death
Mounting the stairway, coming to take my breath.

The River That Floats Friends So Far Apart

I know now but I did not realize then
What this river flowing through this plain
Is, and where it goes and how it flows:

"Where are you going, Walter, when you go?"
"Tripoli for sun, Jungfrau for snow—
It makes no difference; when I go, I go."

Then we planned to meet after a year;
I don't know where he is now, I am here,
Walter may be in Spain or anywhere.

Letters? What are letters? Only paper
And ink borne by small colored stamps that cost
Pence, sous, pfennings, centimes, and are lost

In waste-baskets, and thoughts are only things
That reverberate in memory when it rings.

Life Is Cheap

Life is cheap as reflections upon water,
Life is cheap as shadows upon grass;
If not now, then a day will come to pass
When you will believe me, son and daughter.

Oh, yes, life is precious, you are told.
Ah, yes, life is priceless, people say.
And "Carnegie could not buy it with his gold,"
And no man with his power or his word
Can force the thread of tenuous life to stretch
One inch further for the dying wretch.

So I will not argue but I stoutly claim
That life is cheap, to be bought left and right
For little, life lives on little, day and night,
Cheapness and living are about the same.

The Wind Said

The wind said: What I know is terrible
Enough to know, and still more terrible
To tell; it is of no import, however.

But still an urge to impart it makes me blow
Through apathetic worlds far off and near!

How can I hide my secret or confide
It into worthy ears—if I should speak out
Telling the mordant and the awful truth,
Trees would wither, mountains would crumble away,
And the dust of death would fill the air of day.

I could seize mortals—fill them with my fire—
Let them adopt means they might know to tell—

But what I may know I keep and do not say
Nor ever babble, although water will.

Undecided, the Arguments Persist

Was it hallucination Martin Luther
Saw? I rather doubt it, I would rather
Go on thinking he saw incarnate,
Pulsating there and grim, the ancient Sate.

And did Moses out of sheerest nothing
Make water-honey manna? The mathematician
Wonders how he could have been such a magician;
Already credulity's bird is on the wing.

All one can say is—I choose to believe
Or disbelieve what I hear and not to prove

That the virgin saw (so far as I am concerned)
The announcing angel, that a great sword burned
In front of Adam and Eve, and there was a flood,
And there is a fountain of Emmanuel's blood.

The Faithful Man

I am sure that inexorable laws
Control events for which we know no cause.

I know it likely that infinite gain
Accrues out of the suffering of pain.

I believe that the road that has no end
Leads to the mansion of a certain friend.

I think that the last boundary of space
Is only near a very radiant face.

I feel that loud echoes of the word
Fill the silence when nothing else is heard.

Dawn must be more than the herald light
Of a golden orb, though infinitely bright.

The universe must cancel everything
Not in dominion to the invisible king.

For Each Moth and For Each Star

There is no name for sorrow such as yours;
You walk the world with idle empty hands,
Visiting hopeful lands and hopeless lands,
Returning after a given number of years
To find your own land waiting, the same sky
And sun and moon to mark your moments by,
The same lawn, the same house, the poplar trees,
The same occasional rain, the identical breeze
That years ago you decided to forget.

And why forgetfulness? You remember yet
The reason you took that long road to follow:

It was because you never could attain
The shrine a careless god set in your brain
By error that you had to correct with sorrow.

Name Five Streams from an Alphabet of Rivers

There is the thirsty Amazon, first of all,
With the precipitous plains its waters lave,
And hordes of unclean standing by its shore
Timid at its inspiring depths, not brave;

Then the flat Brazos, rumbling, vapid stream,
Without majesty toward the ocean's feet,
Far from inland its loud currents call
To answer cries unanswered heretofore;

Then the Colorado—what prehistoric men
Now merely bones in glass museum cases
Did it once quench; its banks were cool oases
To what tired travellers in delirious dreams?

One could go on—but rivers do that better,
Alph to Zambesi, one for every letter.

Spring Is Not Far Distant

As dead and dry and gone as anything
That ever lived, the earth awaits the spring.

And bulbs, unresurrected, hold the plot
Of dirt their own as if they had forgot
At Zephyr's summons what they have to do;

In less than a month the sky will turn to blue
That now is pre-blue, and what appears as dead
Will rise and shine and shout, revivified.

I can guess how intricate and hard and long
The process is that apparently unfolds
Lending a pristine brilliance to the air
Making a pageant of remitted song;

Now Erda, waiting, in her breast enfolds
Each tree a poem and every leaf a prayer.

Changing from Karl to Fritz: Her Seventh Station

There was flame within her lambent eyes
Lit from the exclamation of surprise
Her ears one time conveyed into the hall
Of her long memory; then the light footfall
Of Karl, her recent lover, died away.

As to young Fritz now, what was she to say
To her new self or to all her older selves
About the books of him stacked upon the shelves
Of her cognition?
                        Lamely, if at all,
She met the issue. And, as for being wise,
She cared no more than for love—each was a curse.

Wisdom! It told her that from better to worse
Her course had waned as she began to see
More and more of the world's machinery.

Familiar God

O deity, no temple and no fanes
Are yours to visit. In the freezing rains
Of winter I know your wandering. My lord,
No priests before you pile a fatted board
Nor are you crowded out with worshippers;

Your mind is true, your body beautiful,
Your spirit good, the glory of your will
Is free and chaste and valiant and I find
Your songs are only uttered by the wind;

The sea and sky are your ambassadors,
Earth's continents your cornucopias,
Your fire is endless and your name immortal,
Your fingernail a greater miracle
Than Zeus' forehead—O familiar!

Odd Stick, Odd Stone

When time began heredity began:
Odd stick, odd stone, odd dissolute forebear
From whom you inherited your auburn hair,
Odd crab, odd fellow, odd ostrich, and odd Finn,
From whom descended your peculiar skin,

Odd person, leman, yokel, hind, or yeoman,
From them you received, even since time began,
The gifts they handed down from hand to hand,
Such as they were, to last as best they can,
Descending, changing, used from man to man;

They must have come from an ancient melting pot
Deities started boiling, then forgot,
Or were possibly stolen off an altar rude
Of thick stones set within a holy wood.

So in the Dust

In the long census of antiquity
Are to be found the fields, the lists, the mead,
That made so many wish that they were dead
To share them; men have always looked ahead
Or far behind to where the vision dims
And fails upon the shore that memory limns:

Thus in the dust of silent libraries
Sleeping in seclusion on the shelves
Are the books of answers to the queries
Of self made by the supernumerary selves;

In times long ago one asked: *Now can it be*
That I am, that this is so, that this will befall?
Quick were the answers, quick, and indirectly:
Troy's ruins, Pompeii's brothels, China's wall . . .

To the Reader
(*You are the you that poets have addressed*)

‗‗‗‗‗‗‗‗‗‗‗‗‗‗‗‗‗‗‗‗‗‗‗‗‗‗‗‗‗‗‗‗‗‗‗‗

Who is the *you* that poets have addressed?

It is the arm they never have caressed,
It is the breast that never was their breast,
The face adored, disturbing, and distressed.

The tryst deep in the garden of the night,
The walk beside the ocean's morning light,
The rendezvous at full noon in the sight
Of day and the city, never meeting quite.

This is the *you,* these are the sacred *ye,*

Of never-seen accursed immediacy
Of need, in the lonesome hour, of the distracted
Heart to phantom heart or face attracted,
Or fancy's residual when real life is subtracted,
That is the you. At least, it is for me.